Education and Training Policy

Inclusion of Students with Disabilities in Tertiary Education and Employment

OECD

This work is published on the responsibility of the Secretary-General of the OECD. The opinions expressed and arguments employed herein do not necessarily reflect the official views of the Organisation or of the governments of its member countries.

Please cite this publication as:
OECD (2011), *Inclusion of Students with Disabilities in Tertiary Education and Employment*, Education and Training Policy, OECD Publishing.
http://dx.doi.org/10.1787/9789264097650-en

ISBN 978-92-64-09741-4 (print)
ISBN 978-92-64-09765-0 (PDF)

Series: Education and Training Policy
ISSN 1990-150X (print)
ISSN 1990-1496 (online)

Photo credits: Cover © styf - Fotolia.com

Foreword

In 2003, the OECD's Centre for Educational Research and Innovation published a report entitled *Disability in Higher Education*. It revealed a lack of information and data on opportunities for young adults with disabilities to enter tertiary education and employment. This lack of information and data appeared to be a key barrier to developing cost-effective inclusion policies to prepare young adults with disabilities to meet the requirements of tertiary education institutions and the labour market and to empower them to be economically self-sufficient and socially independent.

The main objective of this volume is to analyse policies designed to foster transition to tertiary education and to employment, and to identify factors that facilitate or hinder that transition. It describes trends in terms of transition to tertiary education and looks at the strengths and weaknesses of policies and of support for young adults with disabilities as they move to tertiary education and to employment. It also looks at strategies developed by upper secondary schools and tertiary education institutions to smooth transition. It identifies good practices for empowering young adults with disabilities to access tertiary education and employment and be part of society.

The Czech Republic, Denmark, France, Ireland, Norway and the United States contributed to this publication. They provided a background report describing their transition policies, organised site visits and participated in biannual workshops.

The author of this report is Serge Ebersold, professor at France's Institut national supérieur de formation et de recherche pour l'éducation des jeunes handicapés et les enseignements adaptés (INS HEA), in close collaboration with the countries involved.

100653504

ACKNOWLEDGEMENTS

This study has been carried out under the auspices of the OECD's Education Policy Committee and the Group of National Experts on Special Needs Education and overseen by experts and representatives of the countries participating in the study. The country reports provided invaluable insights into their systems and the challenges faced by young people with disabilities and we would like to warmly thank all the country experts who contributed to this review.

The study would not have been possible without the active support of the United States, in particular through financial support, contributions and technical support from the US Social Security Administration (SSA) and the technical support of the US Department of Education, Office of Special Education and Rehabilitative Services (OSERS). Other participating countries also provided financial support for the study.

The author would like to thank participating countries for their engagement in this project as well as those stakeholders met during the site visits. The author would also like to thank present and former OECD colleagues, and in particular, Bernard Hugonnier, Peter Evans, Deborah Roseveare, Paulo Santiago, Heike-Daniela Herzog, Christine Charlemagne and Cassandra Davis, along with Doranne Lecercle for her editing services.

Table of contents

Tables

Boxes

Executive Summary

Young adults with disabilities, and especially those with learning difficulties, have been going on to tertiary education in increasing numbers over the past decade. More are gaining the prerequisites for tertiary education as policies to promote the inclusion of disabled people developed over the past 20 years bear fruit.

Inclusive policies have increased access to tertiary education

---

The "school for all" approach mobilises financial, technical and human resources to provide students with disabilities equal opportunities on an equal footing with their peers by compensating for the consequences of their disability. More flexible learning environments that can be adapted to the diversity of educational needs, the reduction of dropout rates, and quality assurance policies have all helped to increase the number of students with disabilities able to aspire to tertiary education.

In addition, educational systems are more often being mobilised around students' prospects, with a wider range of educational opportunities beyond upper secondary education, more flexible pathways and measures to assist disadvantaged groups, including disabled pupils and students.

The growing proportion of young adults with disabilities in tertiary education is also a direct result of the strategies adopted by upper secondary schools and tertiary education institutions to build pathways to tertiary education and prepare upper secondary school students to cope with the demands of the transition to adulthood.

Secondary schools generally aim to provide upper secondary school students with disabilities with the information that will allow them to make informed decisions. Less often, they encourage them to plan carefully and early enough their path towards tertiary education. Only a few strategies are designed to prepare students for the experience of tertiary education.

In tertiary education, institutions have designed admission and support strategies for students with disabilities to succeed in their studies and, to a lesser extent, to also be well integrated into the university community. Approaches include linking with services that deal with transport, housing, etc., collaborating with secondary education institutions or offering to map out pathways with students.

Admissions strategies also tend to make students with disabilities responsible for themselves, encouraging them to clarify their particular educational needs at as early a stage as possible. They also provide information and advice to students on courses, their accessibility policy and available support and accommodations. They may involve developing a contract to mobilise actors within the institution around a specific support plan that sets out the objectives, the support and accommodations needed, and implementation provisions.

The quality of the transition process depends on whether the institution promotes an inclusive ethos throughout the university community that allows for mobilising each member of the institution to ensure the success and the inclusion of individual students.

This inclusive ethos can be seen particularly clearly in countries that have adopted an educational approach to disability. This approach focuses on how the institutions' modes of organisation and teachers' pedagogical practices can be adapted to address the rhythms and the needs of students with disabilities. In these countries, institutions tend to see diversity as a source of success for the entire university community, to consider support and accommodations as a way to facilitate the success of every student and to view accessibility as a source of development.

*Transition issues are still a concern for young
adults with disabilities*

Inclusive policies have not always succeeded in ensuring the successful transition of young adults with disabilities. Despite the progress made, young adults with disabilities generally have a harder and bumpier transition to tertiary education than other young adults. Those students with a sensory, motor or mental impairment or psychological problems face particular challenges. Their pathways to tertiary education are also less straightforward and there may be breaks or forced changes of direction along the way.

Young adults with disabilities are also less likely than their non-disabled peers to complete their upper secondary studies successfully, particularly when they have a specific learning difficulty, behavioural difficulties or psychological problems.

Transition policies have significantly expanded opportunities for access to, and success in, tertiary education for young adults with disabilities. But they do not address all the obstacles that students face and do not do enough to provide a continuous and coherent pathway to tertiary education and employment.

Successful transition still depends too much on the resources and the resourcefulness of the individuals concerned and their families. Students with sensory, motor or mental impairments and/or from less fortunate socio-economic backgrounds may be more vulnerable as a result.

Successfully completing tertiary studies is a further challenge for disabled students who may encounter further obstacles during their studies. Moreover, the additional resources allocated to institutions and to young adults with disabilities are not sufficiently linked to preparing for their future social and professional inclusion. As a result young adults with disabilities may remain unemployed or underemployed in spite of easier access to higher education.

*Develop transition policies to safeguard
high-quality pathway opportunities*

It is therefore essential to develop policies that encourage a good transition to tertiary education and to employment if education more broadly is to meet the goals of efficiency and equity by delivering access, success and a promising future for all.

Countries are starting to develop specific transition policies and integrate these into the education system: budgetary pressures have provided added impetus to optimising the planning and steering of inclusive policies and avoiding excessive costs. Nonetheless countries continue to face a range of challenges including how to:

- mobilise stakeholders and systems around the future of young adults with disabilities and prevent them from being irremediably marginalised by discontinuities;

- promote synergies between systems and stakeholders involved in the transition process to ensure continuity and coherence in the career path;

- empower young adults with disabilities and their families to meet the demands of the transition to adulthood and of tertiary education and employment;

- make systems and stakeholders capable of satisfying the requirements imposed by the definition and implementation of transition processes;

- provide the mechanisms and tools necessary for planning policies and monitoring transition processes.

Quality transition policies are needed to give equal opportunities and treatment for young adults with disabilities. They:

- provide young adults with disabilities with the same knowledge and skills as other young adults to the full extent possible;

- furnish them, on the same basis as other young adults, with qualifications recognised by tertiary education institutions and the labour market;

- prevent them from being more exposed than other young adults to being neither in employment nor in education or training;

- offer them the same chances of access to the same quality of employment as young adults without disabilities; and

- give them equal opportunities in terms of the length and quality of transition.

This in turn requires policies that:

- are organised around an educational approach to disability which focuses on the enabling or disabling effect of policies and practices;

- promote a legislative framework that prohibits all forms of discrimination and requires institutions to include transition in annual action plans for each young adult with disabilities;

- ensure that the support offered acts as an incentive for tertiary education and access to employment;

- develop bridges between stakeholders that foster continuity and coherent paths between educational levels and sectors;

- provide education systems with financial and methodological incentives to improve transition strategies and strengthen linkages with their environment, particularly with employers and career services;

- link financial resources more closely to the individual education plan which includes a transition plan;

- are anchored in reliable indicators and statistical data for analysis and evaluation;

- create or improve co-ordination arrangements to facilitate local synergies among stakeholders in the education, employment, social and health sectors;

- improve initial and continuing training for personnel in the education system and provide them with methodological tools and support.

Optimising the transition to tertiary education therefore requires:

- strengthening local synergies among the actors involved in the transition process;

- training actors in the educational system involved in the transition process in order to better prepare young people with disabilities to cope with the demands of tertiary education;

- developing modes of financing that allow young adults with disabilities to cover the extra costs due to their disability, and encouraging schools and tertiary education institutions to support young adults with disabilities during the transition process or/and to ensure that they are supported;

- making available reliable and comparable statistics for effective planning and monitoring of policies and processes;

- developing the services and tools needed to steer transition processes or counter the ineffectiveness of existing ones.

Optimising the transition to tertiary education also requires that schools:

- supply adequate information about the courses proposed by the tertiary education sector and the conditions of access to tertiary education;

- provide support to young adults with disabilities throughout the process;

- strengthen their links with their environment.

An easier transition to tertiary education also requires that admission and support services in tertiary education institutions:

- strengthen their links with secondary education institutions, with the bodies that co-ordinate the education and/or transition process and with services involved in extracurricular issues;

- take an educational approach to disability rather than a diagnostic approach;

- develop admissions strategies that go beyond disseminating information;

- have at their disposal the skills, tools and methodologies needed for assessing, systematically and accurately, the educational needs of students with disabilities and providing high-quality support;

- effectively link admissions strategies to support strategies;

- endeavour to ensure that students with disabilities are capable of making the best possible use of the support provided and of taking charge of their future.

Improve transition to work opportunities

However, access to tertiary education does not necessarily lead to employment. The rate of employment of young adults with disabilities is lower than that of the working population of the same age.

Optimising the transition to employment presupposes that:

- the vocational education and training initiatives undertaken in secondary education to optimise the employability of young adults with disabilities offer a real educational alternative;

- tertiary education institutions attach the same importance to the professional future of students with disabilities as they do for other students;

- tertiary education institutions create sufficiently deep-rooted and formalised links with the economic sphere and the actors involved in active employment policies to be able to make full use of initiatives to encourage firms to recruit workers with disabilities;

- admissions and support services for students with disabilities give greater attention to access to employment in their strategies and work more closely with agencies that assist with job searches for persons with disabilities or job placement agencies.

Chapter 1

Post-school transitions for young adults with disabilities

Access to tertiary education is essential for young adults with disabilities: it boosts their chances of access to employment, their possibilities for inclusion and helps to put the prejudices surrounding impairment in the background. It can take on special meaning for young adults with disabilities in that the transition to adulthood changes the demands on educational systems and the conditions of eligibility for aid and support and creates new responsibilities for these individuals. In addition, the path to tertiary education requires the building of bridges and the creation of local synergies to mobilise actors in educational systems and in social and medical circles. Access to tertiary education also presupposes the existence of procedures for providing support to allow young adults with disabilities to cope with their new responsibilities and to adjust to the demands of tertiary education. In this respect it requires an integrated transition system that can ensure a safe pathway from secondary to tertiary education.

Introduction

This chapter identifies factors that affect the transition to tertiary education and employment for young adults with disabilities, and the good practices needed to offer them equal opportunities in terms of access, success and inclusion. It highlights specific factors linked to the passage to adulthood of young adults with a disability or a specific learning difficulty (see Box 1.1) and the impact, in terms of transition, of the definitions of disability, the eligibility for different forms of support, and the demands placed on young adults with disabilities. It also draws attention to the factors that facilitate the coherence and continuity of pathways through educational levels and sectors and into employment. It stresses in addition core elements that should be considered to allow young adults with disabilities to adapt to the requirements of tertiary education and the labour market, as well as the components of an integrated transition system.

The context

It is not easy to obtain precise information on the number of young adults with a disability or a specific learning difficulty. Participating countries either do not have accurate data on those aged 18-25 years or did not include them in their reports. According to the data supplied by Ireland, there were 393 785 persons with disabilities in that country in 2006, of whom 8.7% were between the ages of 20 and 29 (Central Statistics Office, 2008). In Norway, 11% of all 20-35 year-olds were reported to have a form of disability in 2007, the equivalent of a little over 100 000 persons in this age group (Statistics Norway, 2009).

The Czech Republic had around 1 million persons with disabilities in 2007, or 10% of the total population; 60 621 (5.9% of persons with disabilities) were 15-29 years old (Ministry of Education of the Czech Republic, 2009). According to the 2006 population survey, the United States had 41 259 809 non-institutionalised persons with disabilities (age 5 and older), of whom 1 501 184 were between the ages of 16 and 20 and represented 3.6% of the total population of persons with disabilities (US Census Bureau, 2006).

Data on young adults with disabilities described in the country reports are also lacking or imprecise. In Norway, these young adults have mental health problems (58%), cognitive disorders (36%), impaired mobility (20%), a communication disorder (26%), a breathing problem (20%), a visual impairment (18%), or a sensory impairment (10%) (Statistics Norway, 2009).

In the Czech Republic, these young adults have a physical disability (42.6%), a psychological disorder (37.7%), a metabolic problem (34.4%), a cognitive impairment (14.7%), or a sensory impairment (16.5%) (Ministry of Education of the Czech Republic, 2009). In Ireland, they present a cognitive impairment (34.5%), a specific learning difficulty (31.6%), a psychological disorder (23.3%), or a sensory impairment (14.1%); in addition, 45.7% encountered problems for getting to work or to school (13.3%) or simply venturing outside their home (15.4%) (Central Statistics Office, 2008).

Young adults aged 16-20 years with one or more disabilities surveyed in the United States in 2008 had a visual impairment (17.3%), a hearing impairment (12.2%), a mobility impairment (15.6%), a cognitive impairment (68.9%), a self-care disability (11.6%) or difficulty for living independently (33.9%) (Erickson et al., 2010).

Box 1.1 Methodological considerations

This volume builds on previous OECD work on the transition to working life and higher education and on a literature review on the transition to tertiary education and to employment in the United States, in Germany, in Norway and in the United Kingdom (OECD, 2000, 2003a; Felkendorff and Lischer, 2005; Hvinden et al., 2008; Dyson, 2008; Florian and Rafal, 2008; Ebersold, 2008a). It also relies on the background reports from the Czech Republic, Denmark, France, Ireland, Norway and the United States and on the site visits carried out in 2009.

The term tertiary education involves education offering ISCED 5A courses as well as ISCED 5B courses. Programmes, upper secondary schools and tertiary education institutions described in this volume were either mentioned in countries' background reports or visited during the site visits. However, these programmes and initiatives do not reflect the diversity of initiatives in participating countries to facilitate the transition of young adults with disabilities to tertiary education and to employment. This volume does not claim to reflect the full descriptions contained in the country reports but aims to identify good practices that facilitate the transition to tertiary education and employment

This publication focuses primarily on young adults with disabilities in the period of life at which adolescence ends and they start on the path to adulthood. They need to define what they want to do at the end of their schooling and determine how to achieve their goals and be included into society as adults (Furstenberg et al., 2005). They are in the age bracket at which students normally complete upper secondary school or enter tertiary education.

In order to have a common approach that allows for comparing the rationales underlying policies for young adults with disabilities, the analysis relies on the OECD's grouping of national definitions of disability into three cross-national categories (OECD, 2005):

- Cross-national category A (CNC A) includes students with disabilities or impairments viewed in medical terms as organic disorders attributable to organic pathologies (e.g. in relation to sensory, motor or neurological defects). The educational need is considered to arise primarily from problems attributable to these disabilities.

- Cross-national category B (CNC B) encompasses students with behavioural or emotional disorders or specific learning difficulties. The educational need is considered to arise primarily from problems in the interaction between the student and the educational context.

- Cross-national category C (CNC C) represents students with disadvantages arising primarily from socio-economic, cultural, and/or linguistic factors. The educational need is to compensate for the disadvantages attributable to these factors.

This publication concentrates on young adults who have been granted additional resources designed to meet educational needs arising from an impairment or an illness (CNC A) or a specific learning difficulty (CNC B). It excludes those who receive additional resources as a result of a social disadvantage (CNC C), unless they also have educational needs stemming from an impairment, an illness or a learning difficulty.

The term learning difficulty therefore describes students whose needs arise primarily from problems in the interaction between the student and the educational context (CNC B).

Access to tertiary education: a path towards inclusion

Access to tertiary education is an integral part of the right to education and a major condition for social and professional inclusion. It helps to reduce the burden of prejudice with respect to disability and increases the chances of employment. In 2007, for example, the employment rate of disabled Norwegians with tertiary education was 30% higher than that of persons with disabilities who had left school at the end of compulsory education (Bjerkan *et al.*, 2009);[1] in Ireland the probability of employment among persons with disabilities with a tertiary degree was 5% higher than that of the general working population with a tertiary degree (Gannon and Nolan, 2008). Access to tertiary education enhances the capacity of young adults with disabilities to cope with transitions and prevents those who wish and are able to work from gradually withdrawing from the labour market and becoming exposed to severe forms of marginalisation and poverty (OECD, 2003a, 2003b, 2006, 2008a).

Access to tertiary education is, however, more difficult for young adults with disabilities than for young adults on average. While possession of a secondary education diploma has become the rule in OECD countries in recent decades, this is not the case for young adults with disabilities. Table 1.1 shows that in many countries they have trouble getting into upper secondary school; in the United States, the number of children and teenagers receiving additional human, technical or financial resources for a disability or an illness (CNC A) decreased from 3.11% of the total student body in junior high school to 3.04% in senior high school, and it declined from 7.5% to 6.1% for students receiving additional resources because of a specific learning difficulty. In the Czech Republic, it dropped by 0.8% (from 4% to 3.2%) for students receiving additional resources because of a disability, and by more than 6% (from 6.5% to 0.5%) for those receiving additional resources because of a specific learning difficulty (OECD, 2007a).

According to Ireland's National Disability Authority (NDA), in 2007 slightly over 50% of the Irish working population (15-64 years) with disabilities had no secondary school education; the share was 18.8% for the general population (NDA, 2007) (Figure 1.1). In France, children with a disability or a specific learning difficulty have little chance of going on to upper secondary school: the country report shows that 40% of students with disabilities are placed in special education at the end of primary school, 7% are steered from lower secondary school into special education, and 6% are oriented to special education at the upper secondary level. In 2004, only 26% of persons with a disability in Norway attained a tertiary education level, compared to 33.4% for the general population (Borg, 2008). In the Czech Republic, the rate of persons with disabilities with a basic education is twice as high as that of the total population (see Figure 1.2).

The lack of academic credentials increases the vulnerability of young adults with disabilities, particularly as the level of education is rising among the general population (Figures 1.3 and 1.4). It increases their exposure to unemployment as well as to various forms of vulnerability attributable to recurrent unemployment and to the more acute forms of marginal existence associated with health systems that discourage them from searching for employment (OECD, 2003a, 2003b, 2006; De Stefano and Santamaria, 2006).

---

1.   It is nevertheless important to recognise that, as shown later in this report, young adults with disabilities who have only secondary education may differ in profile and types of disabilities from those who have tertiary education.

Table 1.1. Students in lower secondary education receiving disability-linked additional resources (CNC A)

As a percentage of all students in that phase of education (2003)

	CNC A	
	Lower secondary school	Upper secondary school
Japan	1.30	1.11
Hungary	2.87	0.09
Mexico	0.26	n.d.
Finland	4.76	1.37
Belgium (Flemish Community)	3.70	n.d.
Slovak Republic	3.60	1.75
Chile	1.34	n.d.
Spain	2.55	0.49
United Kingdom (England)	3.45	4.12
Czech Republic	3.96	3.18
United States	3.11	3.04

CNC A = Cross-national category A (see Box 1.1).

Source: OECD (2007), *Students with Disabilities, Learning Difficulties and Disadvantages: Policies, Statistics and Indicators*, OECD, Paris.

Figure 1.1. Education level of persons with disabilities and of the total population in Ireland (2006)

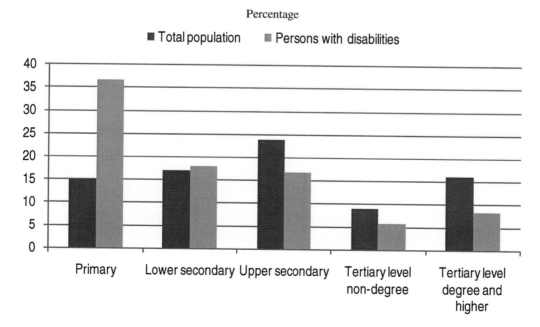

Source: Higher Education Authority (2009), "OECD Project on Pathways for Disabled Students to Tertiary Education and to Employment", Country background report, Department of Education and Skills, Dublin.

Figure 1.2. Education level of persons with disabilities and of the total population in the Czech Republic (2007)

Percentage

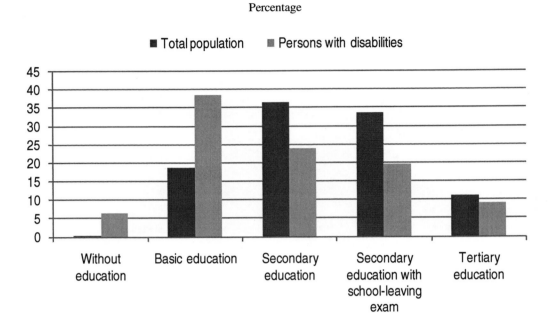

1. The number of persons with no education (0.1% of the total population) is not shown.

Source: Ministry of Education of the Czech Republic (2009), "Transitions to Tertiary Education and to Employment for Young People with Impairments and Learning Difficulties", Country background report, Ministry of Education of the Czech Republic, Prague.

As with health care, individuals' well-being and chances for personal development depend on their access to education. Excluding young adults with disabilities from tertiary education deprives them of the qualifications they need for the labour market, especially in recessions when youth unemployment rises faster than that of the workforce as a whole. To exclude them from tertiary education implies a lack of interest in their chances to engage in international exchanges or in their opportunities to combine courses with a professional activity or internship. Such a lack of interest also leaves unaddressed certain challenges for tertiary education of the Bologna process, such as curriculum diversification, generalisation of lifelong education, and the creation of stronger links to the labour market. In effect it leaves young adults with disabilities more exposed to poverty, and even to crime, and to being irreparably marginalised (Wagner *et al.*, 2005; PMSU, 2005; Aston *et al.*, 2005; Dewson *et al.*, 2004).

Figure 1.3. Employment rate by education level for persons aged 16-30 years in Norway (2006)

Percentage

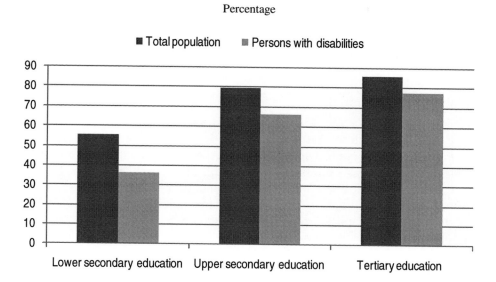

Source: Legard, S. (2009), "Pathways from Education to Work for Young People with Impairments and Learning Difficulties in Norway", Work Research Institute, Oslo.

Figure 1.4. Employment rate for persons with disabilities and for the total population aged 20-34 years in Ireland and in Denmark (2006)

Percentage

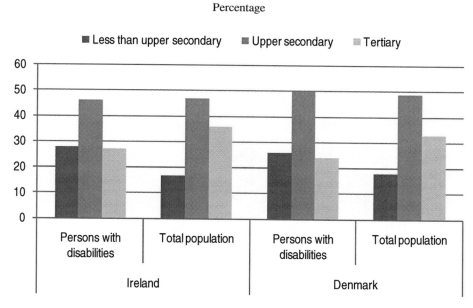

Source: OECD (2008), *Sickness, Disability and Work: Breaking the Barriers: Volume 3: Denmark, Finland, Ireland and the Netherlands*, OECD, Paris.

The challenging transition to tertiary education

Access to tertiary education and employment for young adults with disabilities greatly depends on the capacity of the secondary education system to prepare them for the passage to adulthood. The period beyond upper secondary school constitutes a transition which determines the possibilities for personal growth and for social and professional participation (OECD, 2000; Furstenberg *et al.*, 2005). It captures the passage from adolescence to adulthood, when young adults seek more autonomy, try to distance themselves from the family setting and have to face questions that require them to look both back towards a past for which they must take responsibility and towards a professional and social future that will prepare them for independence. It marks the passage from the status of pupil, whose learning is prescribed and closely supervised, to that of student, who chooses a course of further study in light of his or her interests and professional choices, which often leads to a combination of study and work, sometimes abroad. It means facing a labour market which requires qualities and skills quite different from those required of a pupil at school, and which can be unsettling for those who are not prepared.

New responsibilities to be shouldered

The passage to adulthood can be especially intimidating for those with a disability or a specific learning difficulty. Their capacity to adapt to the demands of tertiary education and employment depends, more than for other young adults, on the availability of appropriate support. Pedagogical differentiation, mobilisation of additional technical, financial and human resources to support them through this period, and special arrangements to facilitate their academic success play an essential role (OECD, 1999).

Yet the conditions that give access to such support are often profoundly modified after secondary school. The requirement of accessibility in tertiary education institutions is conditioned by a specific formal request by individuals with disabilities. In Norway, for example, tertiary education institutions are merely required to make arrangements that are reasonable in the context, unlike primary and secondary schools, which are expected to provide all the conditions that may be necessary to students' success. In the United States, the legal obligation of tertiary education institutions in terms of accessibility depends on individuals' decisions to disclose their disability and needs, whereas schools are required to make the reasonable accommodations deemed appropriate for students with disabilities by the team in charge of their individual education plan (IEP) (Izzo and Lamb, 2002; Stodden *et al.*, 2002).

Access to support ceases to be the responsibility of the school at this point and depends on young adults' ability to demonstrate their needs, to see that these are recognised in terms of their course of study, and to learn about the available support and arrangements. Some young adults, especially those with a specific learning difficulty or a psychological disorder, may not want to reveal that disability, because they fear the consequences of disclosure or because they do not consider themselves "disabled". For example, according to a survey made by Trinity College Dublin, nearly two-thirds of enrolled students with disabilities hesitated to disclose their disability for fear of being stigmatised, or because they felt they did not need special support, or because, having already held a job, they did not consider themselves "disabled". In the United States, 55% of the students enrolled in tertiary education identified by their secondary school as having a disability did not consider themselves to have one by the time they had moved to tertiary education. An additional 8% who considered that they had a disability chose not to disclose it to their tertiary schools (Newman *et al.*, 2009). Such students may deny themselves the special support and accommodation to which they are entitled.

The passage to adulthood may also modify definitions or approaches to disability. Most countries participating in the project no longer define adult disability in terms of academic standards, but instead link it to the standards of the labour market. This is the case in the United States, where the *Individuals with Disabilities Education Act* (IDEA) considers a 3-21 year-old person who needs special education and related services as having a disability. Young adults with disabilities who do not qualify for special education services under IDEA may qualify for special accommodations or modifications under Section 504 of the *Rehabilitation Act* of 1973 and under the *Americans with Disabilities Act* (ADA). Section 504 mainly associates disability with a problem in satisfying educational or professional requirements and the ADA protects individuals with disabilities from discrimination. In Norway, a child's or adolescent's disability is defined as an educational need indicated by the distance separating him/her from the norms of society, which must be closed by special education; for adults, the definition relates to a permanent incapacity to meet personal needs, induced by a reduced capacity to work or by a health problem that precludes employment.

Such changes of definition modify the conditions of eligibility for support and are a source of discontinuity for young adults with disabilities. This may be the case for young adults with a specific learning difficulty who have received support to facilitate their academic success but who, upon becoming adults, are no longer considered eligible in terms of access to employment. In Germany and the United Kingdom, for instance, "educational need" is no longer a formal administrative category once secondary education ends. As a result, young adults with learning difficulties, behavioural disorders or language problems may no longer have access to the support provided for in legislation concerned specifically with persons with disabilities, unless they are enrolled in education or training programmes designed for those leaving special schools (Dyson, 2008; Felkendorff and Lischer 2005). In the United States, under its eligibility criteria, the Social Security Administration provides income support for children with a disability from birth until they reach age 18. At that age, the criteria for eligibility to adult disability benefits change. According to the country report, 33% of child Supplemental Security Income (SSI) recipients with disabilities do not meet the eligibility criteria for adults, and more than half lose all social coverage, are not in tertiary education or employment, or have dropped out of school; a significant percentage have incomes below the poverty level. In Ireland, young adults with disabilities who reach adulthood are no longer assured the support they may have enjoyed throughout their education: only 68.4% of young adults with disabilities applying in 2007-08 for special conditions of access to tertiary education were able to provide sufficient evidence of their disability. In the Czech Republic, young adults with disabilities become recipients of support at age 18, and the modalities of access to resources change significantly, according to the country report.

The disparities between the social treatment of children and of adults with disabilities give the passage to adulthood a very specific nature. They cause changes that require restarting administrative procedures that may be costly in terms of time and energy and can jeopardise access to tertiary education. These changes are a source of discontinuities that may lead to an accumulation of educational and professional experiences that are hard to benefit from on the professional level and may be socially stigmatising (Ebersold, 2001; Caton and Kagan, 2006; Wagner *et al.*, 2006a). Secondary schools must therefore consider the impact of such changes on the academic path of their students and should integrate this in their preparedness strategies; tertiary education institutions should be attentive to the risks of stigmatisation that go with special support and arrangements, which the admissions and support strategies adopted may exacerbate.

Co-operative efforts are needed

The duration of the transition and the itineraries that characterise it are another component of the transition process. In many countries the risk of professional and social exclusion is proportionate to the duration of inactivity after leaving school. In the United States, the chances of success and employment for young Americans with disabilities are better when they move promptly to tertiary education after leaving high school (Newman *et al.*, 2009). As Table 1.2 shows, 22.2% of young adults in Denmark are neither in education nor in employment (NEET) during the first year out of school and 37.2% are in this position after three years. In Ireland, the proportion of young adults considered neither in education nor in employment rises from 19.4% in the first year after leaving school to 23.6% after three years (OECD, 2008b).

**Table 1.2. Status of 15-29 year-olds neither in education nor in employment
one year, three years and five years after leaving school**

Percentage[1]

	Time since end of initial education	Number of observations	Total	Unemployed	Inactive
Denmark	One year	(440)	29.5	7.3	22.2
	Three years	(326)	42.6	5.4	37.2
	Five years and more	(1 480)	22.4	4.2	18.2
Germany	One year	(1 558)	40.7	4.5	36.2
	Three years	(754)	8.7	4.0	4.7
	Five years and more	(4 976)	19.6	7.1	12.5
Ireland	One year	(625)	29.5	10.2	19.4
	Three years	(505)	31.5	7.8	23.6
	Five years and more	(2 571)	25.2	5.8	19.4
Portugal	One year	(756)	30.7	12.3	18.4
	Three years	(729)	15.3	4.6	10.7
	Five years and more	(3 425)	12.0	4.3	7.7

1. Sample restricted to youths aged 15 to 29 years leaving initial education in the years immediately preceding the five-year window of panel survey data used to analyse NEET status.

Source: OECD (2008), *OECD Employment Outlook*, OECD, Paris.

Co-operate to overcome bottlenecks

The bottlenecks that impede continuity and the detours that prolong or change pathways, however, have a particular impact on young adults with disabilities. More than young adults without disabilities, they are exposed to the stigmatising effect of time. Time is, for example, one of the criteria used to assess a person's capacity to progress within a training course, to achieve professional legitimacy, and to take part in the development of society. Tertiary education students who need more time to complete their studies are deemed to have greater difficulty than others and they may face greater obstacles to employment. On the other hand, those who complete their studies within standard time limits may be considered just as capable as others and will be more employable. Those with disabilities are also penalised, pedagogically and socially, by the inaccessibility of education programmes and by ineffective support. This reduces their chances of success and tends to reinforce prejudices and stereotypes about persons with disabilities, because setbacks and taking extra time to enter employment are considered to indicate a lack of ability.

Transition to tertiary education therefore depends on the existence of bridges between successive levels and sectors of education. Young adults with disabilities are more exposed than the average to the discontinuities created by the compartmentalisation of general education and vocational education and training streams (OECD, 2000). In many countries, they tend to pursue training that will not prepare them for tertiary education. In France, high school students with disabilities are proportionally more enrolled in vocational education and training schools or in special vocational training courses within general education (SEGPA), where the chances for academic success and access to tertiary education are lower than in general secondary schools. In Germany the preference given to apprenticeships tends to penalise students who have the skills to go on to upper secondary school (Fasching and Niehaus, 2004). In the United Kingdom, young adults with disabilities are more likely to continue their education after compulsory schooling in the further education sector or in some kind of special provision. They thus embark on courses that are educationally less demanding and more precarious as routes into employment and training (Dyson, 2008). In Norway, only two-thirds of high school students with disabilities hoping for an apprenticeship in the second or third year of secondary school followed their desired course. The remaining third either took another course or dropped out.

The existence of bridges between the general education and the vocational education and training streams can prevent career decisions taken on the completion of secondary education from committing high school students with disabilities to branches or fields of study that might reduce their scope for choice and compromise their access to employment or their professional development. These bridges can also prevent students with disabilities who are enrolled in vocational training courses (*e.g.* apprenticeship or "sandwich" courses) on the completion of lower secondary education from being deprived of opportunities to upgrade their qualifications during working life and enhance their employability (Shavit and Müller, 2000). They reduce the likelihood of failure to which students obliged to change courses because of disability or chronic illness are exposed and which can risk halting or disrupting their progress. And they encourage the smooth continuation of a career path for those wishing to embark on more professionally oriented courses following the completion of lower secondary education (Reiersen, 2004).

Transition opportunities also depend on bridges between the education system, the social services and the health services (EADSNE, 2006). In most countries the responsibility for ensuring institutional accessibility lies with the education system, while the provision of support to compensate for disability falls to the health or social sector. In France, disability compensation is the responsibility of the *conseils généraux* through the departmental offices for persons with disabilities (*Maisons départementales des personnes handicapées,* MDPH), while the educational institutions themselves have to make the arrangements relating directly to the school or university course of study. In the United States, states' rehabilitation agencies are tasked, among other obligations, with providing support to schools, and they must identify existing transition services and help to finance transition services for any young adult with a disability who meets their eligibility criteria. In the Czech Republic, needs identification lies not with the Ministry of Education but with the Ministry of Health, while in Ireland it is the Ministry of Health that assesses educational needs in conjunction with the National Council for Special Education, which co-ordinates the educational process.

Figure 1.5. Support structure for upper secondary students with special education needs in Norway

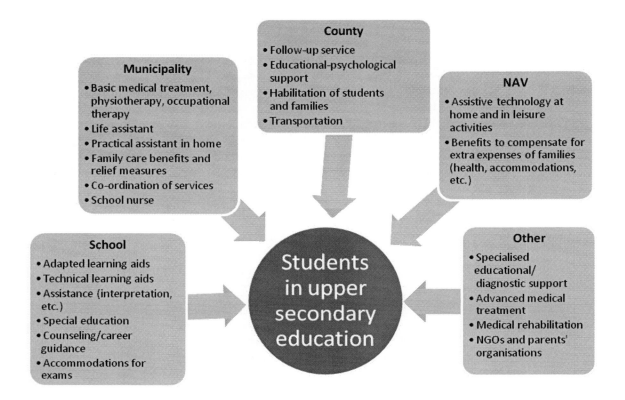

Source: Legard, S. (2009), "Pathways from Education to Work for Young People with Impairments and Learning Difficulties in Norway", Work Research Institute, Oslo.

As indicated in Figure 1.5, Norwegian upper secondary students with disabilities may receive support from five different sources. The educational institution will offer technical aid and pedagogical support as well as any necessary arrangements for examinations, special education and coaching. The municipality is responsible for medical care and assisted living arrangements, family allowances and support, and co-ordination of services. The county provides monitoring services, psychological and educational support, transport, and assessment of students' and families' eligibility. The employment and social protection sector (*Arbeids- og velferdsforvaltningen* – NAV) covers families' extra costs and pays for technological aids required at home or for recreation. Upper secondary school students with disabilities are also eligible for educational and diagnostic support, advanced medical care, functional re-education, and support from associations of parents and of persons with disabilities.

Transition opportunities also depend on the incentive character of modes of funding. In France, interviews show that the efforts of tertiary education institutions for the admission and support of students with disabilities increased when specific funding for this purpose was included in the budget law. In the United States, financial incentives for universities to provide bursaries or loans to students with disabilities overcome the barriers raised by university registration fees. In Denmark, coverage of the costs of the medical certification which young adults with disabilities must have to be legally eligible for support has done much to facilitate access to tertiary education for young adults with specific learning disabilities. However, the absence of financial resources for accessing the medical or paramedical support needed to reconcile study with the constraints of a disability is often an important barrier, as is the absence of financial support for obtaining adapted housing or transport. The absence or inadequacy of bursaries is discouraging for young adults who wish to be independent, particularly if they cannot combine their studies with work.

The strength of such incentives also depends, however, on the bridges between the different sources of financing, as the conditions of eligibility and modes of funding are not always consistent with the requirements of educational pathways. In Norway, for example, young adults with disabilities are eligible for support from the employment and social protection sector (NAV) for four years, yet their studies are likely to take longer for reasons of health or, more frequently, because of the pedagogical inaccessibility of tertiary education institutions. In France, the pace of administrative procedures involved in the attribution of financial aids and support by the Departmental Offices for Persons with Disabilities (MDPH) differs from those of university courses of study, and students as well as universities may face significant delays in support and funding allocation.

Create local synergies

Access to tertiary education and employment depends on the synergies created by the different stakeholders involved in the transition process. These synergies are based on close co-operation between the territorial levels involved in the transition to tertiary education and employment. In France, the education of students with disabilities involves the state, the health insurance system, the *départements*, the regions, and the family allowance funding bodies (*caisses d'allocations familiales*), and their prospects for progressing depend heavily on linkages among these different levels of intervention. The regions are responsible for vocational training and physical accessibility of secondary schools; the *conseils généraux*, at *département* level, are responsible for managing funds allocated to the MDPH by the *Caisse Nationale Solidarité Autonomie* (CNSA) for compensating disability, and university rectors are responsible for making their institutions accessible. The lack of information exchange between the different administrations, particularly when it is not legally authorised, makes it difficult to develop a holistic approach that facilities defining, planning and implementing a person's transition process. Administrative compartmentalisation also works against the mobility that is essential in tertiary education, particularly when changing from one region, *département* or municipality to another. In the United States, young adults with disabilities often receive support in addition to that delivered by schools or universities, and the quality of transition depends on the co-ordinated efforts of specialised educators, non-specialised teachers, community service agencies and occupational rehabilitation agencies (Newman *et al.*, 2009).

These synergies relate to forms of co-operation established between secondary and tertiary education institutions. Where co-operation exists, specific arrangements can be made early in order to meet academic or job requirements and to ensure sufficient continuity so that young adults with disabilities applying for support will not have to justify their disability or problem again. Such links also allow for anticipating the support that may be necessary, the skills required and the conditions for putting them to work. These links may be developed through teaching programmes in which staff are able to mentor students with disabilities, take part in teaching and in certain cases contribute to curricular design. They may be further developed by monitoring students with disabilities who complete secondary education, by appropriately targeted training initiatives for staff involved in both secondary and tertiary education, or by the establishment of multidisciplinary teams responsible for evaluating needs and devising transition procedures. They may also be pursued through bridges created by structures specifically devoted to transition issues, as in Denmark or the United States, or through the offer of postsecondary non-university training to prepare young adults for the demands of tertiary education.

These synergies can also be established through good links between the education sector and the employment sector in order to align young adults' plans and aspirations with the demands of the labour market (McKenzie, 1998). The absence of linkages between schools or universities and the employment sector may deprive persons with disabilities of valuable professional experience and employers of better insight into the potential and abilities of persons with disabilities (Anvik, 2006; Getzel *et al.*, 2001). For example, while schools in the United States generally try to be accessible to students with disabilities, only a quarter of them contact tertiary education institutions, vocational training service providers, or bodies dealing with placement in employment within the framework of the transition plan drawn up with students with disabilities (Florian and Rafal, 2008). A better relation between the education and employment sectors can be achieved through curricula that enable upper secondary school students to combine general education with vocational education and training and gain insight into the world of work, an experience much appreciated by employers (OECD, 2000). It may also take the form of a course of study which includes practical internships or work-study formulas; this incites upper secondary students to integrate a professional element into their career choice and prepares them to put their theoretical knowledge into practice as the situation demands (OECD, 2000; Béduwé and Giret, 2004). This relation can also be ensured through services specifically devoted to steering young adults towards employment and counselling them about access to employment, apprenticeship or vocational training courses.

These synergies also depend on the kinds of co-operation that secondary and tertiary education institutions establish with the family, which can have a direct influence on the student's academic performance and social inclusion (Henderson and Mapp, 2002; James and Partee, 2003; Simon, 2001). Family involvement improves upper secondary students' attendance, their involvement in the schooling process, their academic achievement and, correlatively, reduces the risk of dropout or failure at school (Catsambis and Garland, 1997; Lamorey, 2002; Harry, 2002). Family involvement also helps to compensate for a lack of linkages between sources of financing, to overcome possible discrepancies between different laws and regulations, and to fill the gaps that may exist between the different sectors involved in the transition process.

Facilitating the adjustment to the demands of tertiary education

Transition to tertiary education also depends on the capacity of young adults with disabilities to adjust to the demands of tertiary education and the labour market. This capacity is correlated with the effectiveness of upper secondary school, as university access imposes demands in terms of a diploma, skills or test scores. A student with disabilities has fewer chances of success in secondary school than other students. In Germany, only a few dozen of the 45 000 students with disabilities leaving secondary school each year hold qualifications giving access to tertiary education (Powell *et al.*, 2008); in the United States, despite progress made, their dropout rate is twice as high as that of the student body as a whole, especially when they have an emotional disturbance (National Center on Secondary Education and Transition, 2004; Wagner *et al.*, 2006a).

This capacity for adjustment also depends on the ability of the education system to adapt to the needs and rhythms of students with disabilities who may work at a slower than average pace and whose investment in the class group, motivation for schoolwork and academic performance depend, more than for other students, on the self-assurance that they are able to acquire (OECD, 2007b; McIntosh *et al.*, 1993; Côté, 1996). It is thus essential not to lower the demands made on upper secondary students as compared to those made on students without disabilities but to ensure that the school's pedagogical framework allows them to participate fully in school life. It is necessary to differentiate teaching practices sufficiently, to make course content more easily accessible, and to make the appropriate arrangements for test administration (Gersten, 1998; NCES, 2004; Thurlow *et al.*, 1998; OECD, 1999; Christenson, 2002; Sinclair *et al.*, 1999).

The modes of education offered to children and young adults with disabilities play an essential role in this regard. The chances of continuing to tertiary education are better when they are schooled in a regular class. They are more likely than those schooled in a special school or class to have a course of study conducive to their academic success and their inclusion (Burchardt, 2005; Wagner, 2006b). For example, according to the Norwegian country report, upper secondary school students with disabilities who receive the same instruction as other students, while benefiting from additional resources as necessary, have better academic results than those schooled in special classes and particularly in special schools.

Students with disabilities who receive appropriate instruction in a regular class are keener to go to school and perform better than those who attend a special class or who receive inadequate instruction in a regular class. They are also more likely to feel that they are in good health and to have the relational capacities needed to interact satisfactorily with their classmates. They are more likely to have the social resources that facilitate employment, since school gives them the chance to forge lasting bonds on which they can build social relations that will be useful in their professional and social life. By contrast, students with disabilities who cannot gain entrance to secondary school and who must be educated in a special setting may find themselves trapped in courses of study that do not facilitate academic success and social inclusion. In the United States, special schools may place fewer demands on students than a regular class, and give them higher marks than their performance would merit, at the risk of penalising them academically and professionally (Stodden *et al.*, 2002). In Germany, the chances of success of children schooled in special settings seem lower than for those in mainstream schools: only 0.01% of such students graduated from the school system in 2003 with a diploma that would give access to tertiary education (Kultusministerkonferenz, 2005), and the great majority were deprived of the knowledge and learning available to students in mainstream schools, despite the availability of special pedagogical resources (Wocken, 2000).

Access to tertiary education is not the same in all countries participating in the project. As Figure 1.6 shows, secondary school students in the Czech Republic who receive additional resources for disability (CNC A) are for the most part enrolled in special schools, while in the United States they tend to attend regular or special classes.

Figure 1.6. Secondary education students receiving additional resources for disability (CNC A)

By type of schooling (2003)

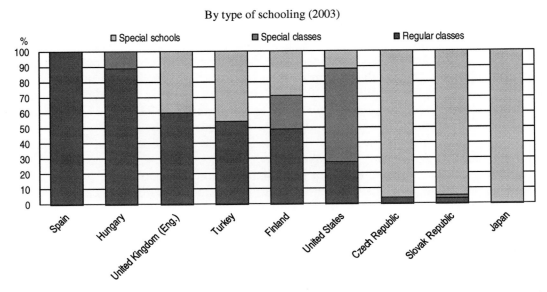

Source: OECD (2007), *Students with Disabilities, Learning Difficulties and Disadvantages: Policies, Statistics and Indicators*, OECD, Paris.

In contrast, as shown in Figure 1.7, American students with a specific learning difficulty (CNC B) receive special education services both in regular and in special classes. Czech students receiving additional resources for a specific learning difficulty are largely accommodated for regular classes.

The capacity of secondary school graduates to adapt to tertiary education and employment will also depend on the self-assurance they have acquired in school and/or through contact with the structures of the transition process (Côté, 1996). This involves the cognitive, emotional, ethical, social and physical skills needed to take decisions, to assume responsibility and to develop the sense of belonging required to interact with others on an equal footing. It provides, according to existing research, skills that are essential to move on to tertiary education (Eccles and Gootman, 2002; Roth and Brooks-Gunn, 2003). Schools may therefore need to encourage young adults with disabilities or specific learning difficulties to identify their preferences regarding their post-school careers, with due regard for their abilities and the corresponding required skills, as well as the professional opportunities they may have (Castellano *et al.*, 2002). It may also be necessary to enable them to overcome problems, take decisions and assume responsibility for themselves, by means of extracurricular activities or artistic, sports or voluntary activities (Larson, 2000; Wehman, 1996). They must be allowed as well to make use of transition periods to acquire skills and faculties that will strengthen their prospects of social and professional inclusion, to develop their self-confidence, to be aware of what is expected of them, and to see themselves as capable of responding to the possible changes and requirements entailed (Shaw, 2007; Jones, 2002).

Figure 1.7. Students receiving additional resources for a specific learning difficulty (CNC B) during compulsory education

By type of schooling (2003)

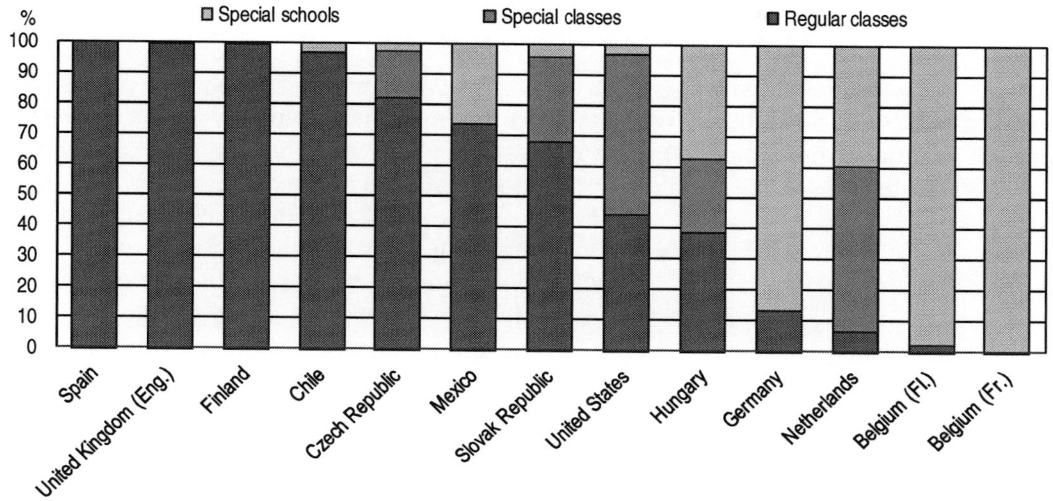

Source: OECD (2007), *Students with Disabilities, Learning Difficulties and Disadvantages: Policies, Statistics and Indicators*, OECD, Paris.

Build integrated systems to safeguard the transition process

Access to tertiary education and to employment after secondary school does not depend solely on the capacity of education systems to be equitable in terms of access and success (Hutmacher *et al.*, 2001). It also depends on the ability to achieve a successful transition by helping students with disabilities to adapt to the changes that are part of the passage to adulthood, by preventing discontinuities and disruptions due to the compartmentalisation of the different levels and sectors of education, and by making it possible for them to satisfy the demands of tertiary education and the labour market. It requires paying close attention to the conditions of their progress towards tertiary education and employment, beyond simply informing them about existing opportunities, the jobs for which their studies will prepare them, and the requirements they will have to face by entering a new level of education.

It is necessary to place young adults with disabilities on an equal footing with young adults without disabilities in terms of:

- having, as far as possible, the same knowledge and skills;

- possessing, like their peers, qualifications that are recognised by tertiary education or employment;

- not being more exposed to being NEET;

- having the same chances of accessing a job of equal quality;

- not facing steeper or rockier pathways.

Ensuring a successful transition requires early planning to help young adults with disabilities and their families to make enlightened choices about their future, as pointed out by the National Council for Special Education in Ireland following a series of studies. It also requires co-ordinated action throughout the process on the part of the parties involved in the student's career, as noted in the definition of IDEA transition services adopted in the 1990 amendment of IDEA in the United States. It depends in addition on the ability acquired by young adults with disabilities to cope with the changes involved in the passage to adulthood and on their belief in that ability.

An integrated transition system can help ensure a successful transition and prevent young adults with disabilities from the kinds of marginality and exclusion to which inactivity would expose them. It must be based on an education system that includes students' future in its missions and on education strategies that include their possibilities for social and professional participation once they have completed their schooling and received their diploma. This means giving young adults with disabilities the same opportunities to enter education programmes as their peers without disabilities and the same chances of success at all levels of schooling, so that they are ready for the academic demands of tertiary education institutions. Schools must be encouraged to view the pedagogical environment in light of students' itineraries, to mobilise local stakeholders and families, to reinforce their inclusion at the local level, and to develop warning systems to help keep students from abandoning their studies.

This integrated transition system takes an educational perspective that views disability, as suggested by the World Health Organization (WHO), in terms of the interaction between the individual, the constraints and possibilities imposed by the impairment, and the forms of support offered by the environment, rather than as an intrinsic characteristic of the individual. From this perspective, any person who does not receive the support that allows him or her to learn and to develop is in a sense "disabled". It focuses on the ability of education systems to help children and adolescents to move beyond their disability and achieve their full potential, and thus contributes to the continuity of the path they take (UNESCO, 1994; WHO, 2001; Ebersold, 2008b).

An integrated transition system presupposes the availability of co-ordinated financial, technical and human support to ensure equality of opportunity for young adults with disabilities in terms of access and progress, during their education and during the various stages of the transition process. This support may be informal and provided by students with disabilities and by their families. For this reason, they should be involved in defining the transition process and in its implementation. Support may also be more formal, provided by professional staff responsible for counselling and assistance in educational institutions as well as by other professionals specifically concerned with working out and implementing the transition process.

An integrated transition system also assumes the existence of guidance services and tools for linking the different levels and sectors of intervention as well as the different levels of education and of the bridges essential to ensure continuity and coherence. It is essential to have indicators that encourage the players involved to consider transition in the light of its real value and to have statistics which can be used to monitor individuals' paths, identify aspects conducive to the continuity and consistency of routes through education and towards employment, to fully understand the factors that impede progress in education and the social inclusion of young adults with disabilities, as well as to appreciate the positive or negative impact of policies and practices. Longitudinal studies following cohorts of individuals over a certain period of time are an essential tool here.

Such an integrated transition system can be organised within an institutional framework dedicated to transition that is able to create an environment favourable to continuity. As in the United Kingdom, such a framework can take the form of specific structures designed to support institutions, young adults with disabilities and their families in preparing and implementing a transition plan. It can also take the form, as in the United States, of a body at municipal level, which brings together the partners needed for effective collaboration on transition planning, with equal representation of administrators, staff members, families and users. These bodies share financing programmes, develop policies and co-operation agreements on forms of co-operation, and advise young adults with disabilities and their families about existing services.

This institutional framework seems essential for equipping stakeholders to take innovative action. It can help to mobilise members of the education system around students' future by encouraging them to be open to their environment or by establishing linkages among the different stakeholders in the transition process (Dee, 2006). It may also contribute to putting young adults with disabilities in a position to satisfy the demands of tertiary education and employment by developing strategies that will give them the skills, the behaviour and the attitudes needed to learn and to build their future, to gear their expectations and their desires to their personal strengths, to participate actively in community life, and to take knowledgeable decisions. These transition services can also help young adults with special education needs see themselves as capable of coping with the demands imposed by the many changes along the road to adulthood, so that they feel entitled to participate in economic and social life on an equal footing with all.

Conclusion

The conditions for entering tertiary education are different for young adults with disabilities than for other young adults. Unlike the latter, they need to be informed about the accessibility of tertiary education institutions and to make their educational needs known in order to receive the support and accommodations to which they are entitled. The continuity of their path depends on the manner in which upper secondary schools prepare them for the new responsibilities they must take on and include in their preparation strategies changes that may occur during the passage to adulthood in terms of access to support or the definition of disability. It also depends on the way in which tertiary education institutions inform them about course requirements and guidance opportunities and encourage them to disclose their special needs.

Unlike those of other young adults, their pathway opportunities may encounter bottlenecks that may hinder their progress or impose detours that may overexpose them to unemployment and exclusion. The continuity and coherence of their pathways therefore depend on bridges between secondary and tertiary education and the world of work made possible by local synergies developed by stakeholders involved in the transition process.

Transition to tertiary education and to employment thus calls for integrated transition systems able to ensure effective paths at the end of secondary education and education systems that are equitable in terms of access, success and inclusion.

References

Anvik, C.H. (2006), *Mellom drøm og virkelighet? Unge funksjonshemmede i overganger mellom utdanning og arbeidsliv*, NF-rapport No. 17, Bodø, Nordlandsforskning.

Aston, J. *et al.* (2005), *Post-16 Transitions: A Longitudinal Study of Young People with Special Educational Needs (wave three)*, Research Report RR655, DfES.

Béduwé, C. and J.F. Giret (2004), "Le travail en cours d'études a-t-il une valeur professionnelle?" *Économie et statistiques*, No. 378-379.

Bjerkan, K.Y., M. Veenstra and J. Eriksen (2009), "Levekårene blant unge voksne: bedring, men godt nok?", Paper presented at the Konferanse om levekårene for personer med nedsatt funksjonsevne.

Borg, E. (2008), Funksjonshemming og arbeidsmarkedet: om betydningen av utdanning for yrkesaktivitet, *Tidsskrift for velferdsforskning,* Vol. 11(2), pp.83-95.

Burchardt, T. (2005), *The Education and Employment of Disabled Young People – Frustrated Ambition,* Joseph Rowntree Foundation, The Policy Press, London.

Castellano, M. *et al.* (2002), "Career and Technical Education Reforms and Comprehensive School Reforms in High School: Their Impact on Education Outcomes for At-Risk Youth", *The Highlight Zone: Research@Work No. 8*, National Research Center for Career and Technical Education, University of Minnesota, St.Paul, MN.

Caton, S. and C. Kagan (2006), "Tracking Post-School Destinations of Young People with Mild Intellectual Disabilities: The Problem of Attrition", *Journal of Applied Research in Intellectual Disabilities*, Vol. 19, pp. 143-152.

Catsambis, S. and J.E. Garland (1997), *Parental Involvement in Students' Education during Middle School and High School,* CRESPAR Report 18, Johns Hopkins University, Baltimore, MD.

Central Statistics Office (2008), *National Disability Survey 2006 – First Results,* Dublin Stationery Office.

Christenson, S. (2002), "Check and Connect: A Model to Enhance Student Engagement and Prevent Dropout", Paper presented at the meeting of the National Dropout Forum, Washington, DC.

Côté, J.E. (1996), "Sociological Perspectives on Identity Formation: The Culture Identity Link and Identity Capital", *Journal of Adolescence*, No. 19.

De Stefano, G. and C. Santamaria (2006), *Tableau de bord sur l'emploi et le chômage des personnes handicapées*, ministère de l'Emploi, de la Cohésion sociale et du Logement, Paris.

Dee, L. (2006), *Improving Transition Planning for Young People with Special Educational Needs,* Open University Press, Maidenhead.

Dewson, S. *et al.* (2004), *Post-16 Transitions: A Longitudinal Study of Young People with Special Educational Needs.* Wave two, DfES, London.

Dyson, A. (2008), "Transitions for Disabled and Vulnerable Young People in the United Kingdom", Background paper for the OECD, University of Manchester.

Ebersold, S. (2001), *L'invention de l'inemployable ou l'insertion aux risques de l'exclusion,* PUR, Rennes.

Ebersold, S. (2008a), "Pathways for People with Disabilities Towards Tertiary Education and Employment: Preliminary Findings from a Literature Review Covering Selected OECD Countries", OECD.

Ebersold, S. (2008b), "Adapting Higher Education to the Needs of Disabled Students: Developments, Challenges and Prospects", in OECD, *Higher Education to 2030, Volume 1: Demography*, OECD, Paris.

Eccles, J. and J.A. Gootman (eds.) (2002), *Community Programs to Promote Youth Development,* Board on Children, Youth and Families, Division of Behavioral and Social Sciences and Education, National Research Council and Institute of Medicine, National Academy Press, Washington, DC.

Erickson, W., C. Lee and S. von Schrader (2010), *2008 Disability Status Report: The United States,* Cornell University Rehabilitation Research and Training Center on Disability Demographics and Statistics, Ithaca, NY.

European Agency for Development in Special Needs Education (EADSNE) (2006), *Individual Transition Plans, Supporting the Move from School to Employment,* European Commission, Brussels.

Fasching, H. and M. Niehaus (2004), "Berufliche Integration von Jugendlichen mit Behinderungen: Synopse zur Ausgangslage an der Schnittstelle von Schule und Beruf", *Berufs- und Wirtschaftspädagogik – online 6, www.bwpat.de.*

Felkendorff, K. and E. Lischer (eds.) (2005), *Barrierefreie Übergänge? Jugendliche mit Behinderungen und Lernschwierigkeiten zwischen Schule und Berufsleben,* Pestalozzianum, Zürich.

Florian, L. and J. Rafal (2008), "Transitions of People with Disabilities Beyond Secondary Education in the United States", Background paper for the OECD, University of Aberdeen and Cambridge University.

Furstenberg, F.F., R.G. Rumbaut and R.A. Settersten (2005), *On the Frontier to Adulthood,* University of Chicago Press, Chicago, IL.

Gannon, B. and B. Nolan (2008), *Disability and Social Inclusion in Ireland,* National Disability Authority, Dublin.

Gersten, R. (1998), "Recent Advances in Instructional Research for Students with Learning Disabilities: An Overview", *Learning Disabilities Practice,* Vol. 13(3), pp. 162-170.

Getzel, E.E., R.A. Stodden and L.W. Briel (2001), "Pursuing Postsecondary Education Opportunities for Individuals with Disabilities", in P. Wehman (ed.), *Life Beyond the Classroom: Transition Strategies for Young People with Disabilities,* Paul H. Brookes Publishing Co., Baltimore, MD.

Harry, B. (2002), "Trends and Issues in Serving Culturally Diverse Families of Children with Disabilities", *Journal of Special Education,* Vol. 36(3), pp. 131-138.

Henderson, A.T. and K.L. Mapp (2002), *A New Wave of Evidence: The Impact of School, Family, and Community Connections on Student Achievement,* Southwest Educational Development Laboratory, National Center for Family and Community Connections with Schools, Austin, TX.

Higher Education Authority (2009), "OECD Project on Pathways for Disabled Students to Tertiary Education and to Employment", Country background report, Department of Education and Skills, Dublin.

Hutmacher, W., D. Cochrane and N. Bottani (eds.) (2001), *In Pursuit of Equity in Education – Using International Indicators to Compare Equity Policies,* Kluwer Academic Publishers, Dordrecht/Boston/London.

Hvinden, B. *et al.* (2008), "Thematic Review of the Transition of People with Disabilities Beyond Secondary Education", Background paper for the OECD, Nova, Oslo.

Izzo, M. and M. Lamb (2002), "Self-Determination and Career Development: Skills for Successful Transitions to Postsecondary Education and Employment", *www.nceset.hawaii.edu/Publications/index.html#papers*, accessed 28 July 2003.

James, D.W. and G. Partee (2003), *No More Islands: Family Involvement in 27 School and Youth Programs,* American Youth Policy Forum, Washington, DC.

Jones, G. (2002), *The Youth Divide: Diverging Paths into Adulthood,* Joseph Rowntree Foundation, YPS, York.

Kultusministerkonferenz (2005), "Sonderpädagogische Förderung in Schulen 1994 bis 2003", *Statistische Veröffentlichungen der Kultusministerkonferenz,* Vol. 177, Kultusministerkonferenz, Bonn.

Lamorey, S. (2002), "The Effects of Culture on Special Education Service: Evil Eyes, Prayer Meetings, and IEPs", *Teaching Exceptional Children*, Vol. 34(5), pp. 67-71.

Larson, R.W. (2000), "Toward a Psychology of Positive Youth Development", *American Psychologists,* Vol. 55(1), pp. 170-183.

Legard, S. (2009), "Pathways from Education to Work for Young People with Impairments and Learning Difficulties in Norway", Work Research Institute, Oslo.

McIntosh, R. *et al.* (1993), "Observation of Students with Learning Disabilities in General Education Classrooms", *Exceptional Children*, Vol. 60(3), pp. 249-261.

McKenzie, P. (1998), "The Transition from Education to Work in Australia Compared to Selected OECD Countries", paper delivered to the 6th International Conference on Post-compulsory Education and Training, Gold Coast, Queensland, December.

Ministry of Education of the Czech Republic (2009), "Transitions to Tertiary Education and to Employment for Young People with Impairments and Learning Difficulties", Country background report, Ministry of Education of the Czech Republic, Prague.

National Center for Education Statistics (NCES) (2005), *Career Technical Education Statistics*, US Department of Education, Washington, DC.

National Center on Secondary Education and Transition (2004), *Current Challenges Facing the Future of Secondary Education and Transition Services for Youth with Disabilities in the United States*, US Department of Education, Office of Special Education Program, Washington, DC.

National Disability Authority (NDA) (2007), *A Strategy of Engagement Towards a Comprehensive Employment Strategy for People with Disabilities*, Dublin.

Newman, L. *et al.* (2009), *The Post-High School Outcomes of Youth with Disabilities up to 4 Years After High School*, SRI International, Menlo Park, CA.

OECD (1999), *Inclusive Education at Work: Students with Disabilities in Mainstream Schools*, OECD, Paris.

OECD (2000), *From Initial Education to Working Life: Making Transitions Work*, OECD, Paris.

OECD (2003a), *Disability in Higher Education*, OECD, Paris.

OECD (2003b), *Transforming Disability into Ability: Policies to Promote Work and Income Security for Disabled People*, OECD, Paris.

OECD (2005), *Students with Disabilities, Learning Difficulties and Disadvantages: Statistics and Indicators*, OECD, Paris.

OECD (2006), *Sickness, Disability and Work: Breaking the Barriers, Volume 1: Norway, Poland and Switzerland*, OECD, Paris.

OECD (2007a), *Students with Disabilities, Learning Difficulties and Disadvantages: Policies, Statistics and Indicators*, OECD, Paris.

OECD (2007b), *Understanding the Social Outcomes of Learning*, OECD, Paris.

OECD (2008a), *Sickness, Disability and Work: Breaking the Barriers, Volume 3: Denmark, Finland, Ireland and the Netherlands*, OECD, Paris.

OECD (2008b), *OECD Employment Outlook*, OECD, Paris.

Powell, J.J.W., K. Felkendorff and J. Hollenweger (2008), "Disability in the German, Swiss and Austrian Education Systems", in S.L. Gabel and S. Danforth, *Disability and the Politics of Education*, Peter Lang, New York.

Prime Minister's Strategy Unit (PMSU) (2005), *Improving the Life Chances of Disabled People*, Final Report, Prime Minister's Strategy Unit, London.

Reiersen, T. (2004), *Oppfølgingsundersøkelse av arbeidssøkere som sluttet å melde seg ved Aetat høsten 2002*, Del 2: Yrkeshemmede arbeidssøkere.

Roth, J.L. and J. Brooks-Gunn (2003), "Youth Development Programs: Risk Prevention and Policy", *Journal of Adolescent Health*, Vol. 32, pp. 170-182.

Shavit, Y. and W. Müller (2000), "Vocational Secondary Education. Where Diversion and Where Safety Net?", *European Societies,* Vol. 2(1), pp. 29-50.

Shaw, S. (2007), "Postsecondary Education", in L. Florian (ed.), *The Sage Handbook of Special Education,* Sage, London.

Simon, B.S. (2001), "Family Involvement in High School: Predictors and Effects", *NASSP Bulletin*, Vol. 85(627), pp. 8-19.

Sinclair, M.F. *et al.* (1999), "Dropout Prevention for Youth with Disabilities: Efficacy and Sustained School Engagement Procedure", *Exceptional Children*, Vol. 65(1), pp. 7-21.

Statistics Norway (2009), *Fakta om utdanning I Norge 2009: nokkeltall fra 2007,* Statistic sentralbyra, Oslo.

Stodden, R., M.A. Jones and K.B.T. Chang (2002), "Services, Supports and Accommodations for Individuals with Disabilities: An Analysis across Secondary Education, Postsecondary Education and Employment", Unpublished manuscript, Honolulu.

Thurlow, M.L., J.L. Elliott and J.E. Ysseldyke (1998), *Testing Students with Disabilities: Practical Strategies for Applying with District and State Requirements,* Corwin Press, Thousand Oaks, CA.

UNESCO (1994), *The Salamanca Statement and Framework for Action*, UNESCO, Paris.

US Census Bureau (2006), *American Community Survey,* Washington, DC.

Wagner, M. *et al.* (2005), *After High School: A First Look at the Postschool Experiences of Youth with Disabilities:* A *report from the National Longitudinal Transition Study-2 (NLTS2)*, SRI International Menlo Park, CA.

Wagner, M. *et al.* (2006a), *An Overview of Findings From Wave 2 of the National Longitudinal Transition Study-2 (NLTS2),* SRI International, Menlo Park, CA.

Wagner, M. *et al.* (2006b), *The Academic Achievement and Functional Performance of Youth with Disabilities. A Report of Findings from the National Longitudinal Study-2 (NLTS2)*, SRI International, Menlo Park, CA.

Wehman, P. (1996), *Life Beyond the Classroom: Transition Strategies for Youth with Disabilities,* SRI International, Menlo Park, CA.

World Health Organization (WHO) (2001), *International Classification of Functioning, Disability and Health,* World Health Organization, Geneva.

Wocken, H. (2000), "Leistung, Intelligenz und Soziallage von Schülern mit Lernbehinderungen", *Zeitschrift für Heilpädagogik*, Vol. 12, pp. 492-503.

Chapter 2

Access to tertiary education is still challenging

The inclusive policies developed in recent years have helped to optimise access to tertiary education for young adults with disabilities, particularly those with learning difficulties. They have facilitated their access to secondary education and their success at school by mobilising the financial, technical and human resources needed to meet their particular educational needs and by developing educational systems that seek to ensure the success of every student regardless of his or her particularities. However, access to tertiary education for young adults with disabilities is not as smooth as it is for other young adults, particularly for those with psychological or behavioural problems. These difficulties are attributable in particular to a lack of synergies between the actors involved in the process of transition to tertiary education, the lack of training of these actors, and the inadequacies of the tools and statistical data required for the development of integrated systems of transition.

Introduction

This chapter describes developments in terms of access to tertiary education in light of initiatives taken in recent years to improve schooling for children with disabilities. It describes the factors that have contributed to these developments, based on an analysis of the country reports and information gathered during the site visits. It also describes the challenges to be taken into account to ensure that access to tertiary education and employment for young adults with disabilities is approached as part of an integrated transition system.

A lack of reliable statistical data

Precise tracking of changes in access to tertiary education for young adults with disabilities is difficult: the data supplied by countries participating in the project are unclear as to the population groups covered, their trajectories and the courses of study followed. Few countries, in fact, have statistics that offer an accurate view of the number of children and young adults with disabilities. Countries such as Norway and Denmark are prohibited by law from identifying persons with disabilities in terms of a disability category, while in the Czech Republic the Statistics Office is not authorised to collect data on students who are disadvantaged or have special learning needs. In the United States, NLTS2 data provide information on participation rates in tertiary education for young adults with disabilities.

The data available show the number of persons using services for persons with disabilities, those receiving support and/or those who feel disabled or consider themselves as such. The data may therefore fail to include young adults who have a disability without having any educational needs, those who require support but do not feel disabled or those who need support but do not satisfy the eligibility criteria. Students whose difficulties are not clearly identified may be counted as having a disability. The issue of the increasing number of dyslexic students in many OECD countries, for example, is surrounded by uncertainties: research is unable to establish whether the increase is attributable to a greater prevalence of dyslexic children, to a steady rise in the number of dyslexic students enrolled in education, to greater responsiveness to dyslexia on the part of schools as a result of the policies implemented, or to the impact of identification methods based on individual subjectivity and the evaluation criteria established by schools (Dyson, 2008; PricewaterhouseCoopers, 2007).

The data included in the country reports also differ. The time periods covered are not always the same, the data may be drawn from different sources, and populations are not always comparable. In countries such as France, the United States and the Czech Republic, the data reflect the number of students declaring an impairment, a long-term illness, or a specific learning difficulty when applying for the support or accommodation required by law. They do not include young adults who do not think it useful or desirable to report their particular circumstances and they do not always show whether young adults are receiving support. In Denmark, the data supplied relate to students receiving support or special accommodation in their course of study. They do not include those who have a disability, a long-term illness or a specific learning difficulty but who receive no support or accommodation, either because they are not eligible or because they have not considered it useful or desirable to declare their educational need. Moreover, the data may count the same student more than once if that person is eligible for several kinds of support. The Irish data refer to the number of students recognised as eligible for the support and accommodations stipulated by law.

In Germany, the data reflect the number of students declaring a health problem or a long-term illness. They were gathered during a 2006 survey conducted by the Ministry of Education and Research among the student population as a whole. They exclude students with an unreported health problem or those who did not consider their disability to be associated with a health problem. This health problem or long-term illness does not necessarily affect their academic progress. According to the 2006 German survey on students in tertiary education, 44% of students reporting a health problem considered that it limited the pursuit of their studies, especially among those with a psychological disorder (91%), problems of the nervous system (70%), reduced mobility (60%) or visceral or metabolic impairments (53%) (Bundesministerium für Bildung und Forschung, 2007).

Easier access to tertiary education

Although the data are not very precise, all countries reported a significant increase in the number of students with disabilities enrolled in tertiary education (Figure 2.1). In the United States, the proportion of young adults pursuing their education after high school increased by 17% between 1987 and 2003, while the proportion of students reporting a disability who were enrolled in tertiary education rose from 9.2% in 1996 to 10.8% in 2007 (Wagner *et al.*, 2005; National Center for Education Statistics, 2009). In Germany, the proportion of students reporting a health problem increased from 15% to 18.5% of the student population between 2003 and 2006 (Bundesministerium für Bildung und Forschung, 2007). In France, the number of students reporting a disability in tertiary education doubled between 2000 and 2006 to 0.4% of the student population (ministère de l'Enseignement supérieur et de la Recherche, 2010). According to the Danish report, the number of students receiving support in tertiary education rose from 0.5% to 0.7% of the student population between 2004 and 2006 (Danish Ministry of Education and Rambøll Management, 2009).

In Norway, the proportion of persons with a disability aged 16-67 years enrolled in tertiary education rose by 7% between 2001 and 2004, and the "living conditions survey" conducted in 2005 revealed that 24% of Norwegian tertiary education students said they had a health problem. Among these, 42% considered that their health problem diminished their ability to study (Statistics Norway, 2007). The number of Czech students with disabilities enrolled in postsecondary vocational training courses increased by 0.02% between 2005 and 2008 to 0.09% of students in these courses. A 2005 survey by the Federation of Persons with Disabilities, covering 161 university faculties, counted 460 students, representing 0.4% of the student body, with a disability (Ministry of Education of the Czech Republic, 2009).

There are few data available to distinguish students with disabilities from the rest of the student population. Those that exist suggest, in line with the work conducted in the context of PISA on pupils with disabilities (OECD, 2007), that the social and demographic characteristics of students' families have a greater influence on their access to tertiary education than in the case of other students. In Norway, parents' educational level plays a more important role for students with disabilities than it does for the average of the population (Bjerkan and Veenstra, 2008). In the United States, young adults with disabilities from the wealthier socio-economic groups are twice as likely to be enrolled in tertiary education as those from a lower socio-economic background (Newman *et al.*, 2009).

Figure 2.1. Students with disabilities enrolled in tertiary education

As a share of total students enrolled

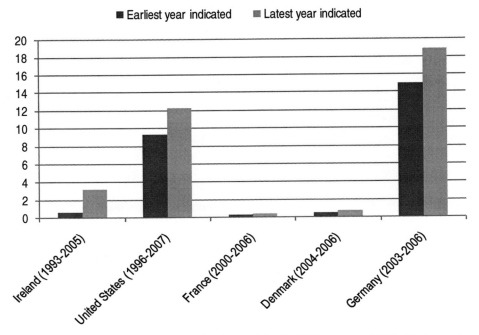

Source : Denmark: Danish Ministry of Education and Rambøll Management (2009), "Pathways for Disabled Students to Tertiary Education and Employment", Country background report, Copenhagen; France: Délégation ministérielle à l'emploi des personnes handicapées (2009), "Parcours des personnes handicapées vers l'enseignement supérieur et vers l'emploi", Rapport de pays, ministère de l'Éducation nationale, Paris; Ireland: Higher Education Authority (2009), "OECD Project on Pathways for Disabled Students to Tertiary Education and to Employment", Country background report, Department of Education and Skills, Dublin; Germany: Bundesministerium für Bildung und Forschung (2007), *Die wirtschaftliche und soziale Lage der Studierenden in der Bundesrepublik Deutschland 2006*; 18. Sozialerhebung des Deutschen Studentenwerks durchgeführt durch HIS Hochschul-Informations-System, Bonn/Berlin; United States: National Center for Education Statistics (2009), *Digest of Education Statistics*, US Department of Education, Washington, DC.

Students with disabilities also appear on the whole to be older than the student average, as shown in Norway's 2005 living conditions survey, while in Ireland the data gathered by universities such as Trinity College Dublin show that many students with disabilities were employed before being enrolled.

As Table 2.1 shows, the profile of students with disabilities enrolled in tertiary education differs among countries. In France, the majority of students with disabilities recruited in 2006 indicated a sensory or physical impairment (44.5%), a health problem (20.6%) or a specific learning difficulty (11.8%). These profiles contrast with those observed in Ireland where 67.1% of the students with disabilities had learning difficulties and in Denmark where 66% of those receiving educational support owing to a disability have a specific learning difficulty (reading and writing). Students with disabilities enrolled in postsecondary vocational training courses in the Czech Republic reported for the most part either a specific learning difficulty (32%) or a mobility impairment (28%). In the United States, undergraduate students with disabilities enrolled in tertiary education in 2003 reported mainly a mobility impairment (25.3%), mental health problems (21.9%), learning difficulties, attention deficit disorders (18.4%) or health problems (17.4%) (Horn and Nevill, 2006). In Germany, a survey in 2006 found that more than 60% of students indicated health problems (Bundesministerium für Bildung und Forschung, 2007).

Table 2.1. Students with disabilities enrolled in tertiary education, by type of disability

Percentage

	Denmark	France	Ireland	United States
	2006	2006	2007	2003
Specific learning difficulty[1]	66.0	8.2	67.1	18.4
Mobility impairment	17.2	20.3	7.7	25.3
Hearing impairment	5.4	10.8	5.2	4.9
Visual impairment	5.4	13.9	3.5	3.8
Health problems		20.1	5.2	17.4
Mental health problems	4.3	11.2	3.1	21.9
Multiple impairments			4.0	
Temporary illness		5.3		
Communication				0.4
Other	1.7	10.2	4.2	7.9
Total	100.0	100.0	100.0	100.0

Note: Denmark: students receiving special education support; France: students who declared a disability; Ireland: students who disclosed a disability; United States: students who declared a disability.

1. This category corresponds to the OECD cross-national category B.

Source : Denmark: Danish Ministry of Education et Rambøll Management, (2009), "Pathways for Disabled Students to Tertiary Education and Employment", Country background report, Copenhagen; France: Délégation ministérielle à l'emploi des personnes handicapées (2009), " Parcours des personnes handicapées vers l'enseignement supérieur et vers l'emploi", Country background report, Ministère de l'Éducation nationale, Paris; Ireland: Higher Education Authority (2009), "OECD Project on Pathways for Disabled Students to Tertiary Education and to Employment", Country background report, Department of Education and Skills, Dublin; United States: Horn and Nevill (2006), *Profile of Undergraduates in U.S. Postsecondary Education Institutions: 2003–04: With a Special Analysis of Community College Students* (NCES 2006-184), US Department of Education, National Center for Education Statistics, Washington, DC.

Finally, transition to tertiary education is not considered in the same way in all countries. In France and the Czech Republic, it essentially concerns young adults with a visible disability, who may require relatively complex support involving pedagogical adaptations but also material arrangements to ensure their mobility both to and on campus or co-ordination of support for daily living (home assistance) and for study. In other countries, transition essentially concerns young adults whose problem is a specific learning difficulty that is not apparent and not always readily accepted as a disability by members of the university community. Such a disability requires pedagogical arrangements that are available only if the student indicates his or her particular need.

Inclusion policies increase acceptance of disability

The growing receptivity of tertiary education to students with disabilities reflects the increasing numbers of students enrolling in tertiary education in OECD countries. As Figure 2.2 indicates, entry rates in tertiary-type A education increased by nearly 20 percentage points on average in OECD countries between 1995 and 2007 (OECD, 2009a).

Figure 2.2. Entry rates into tertiary-type A education (1995, 2000 and 2007)

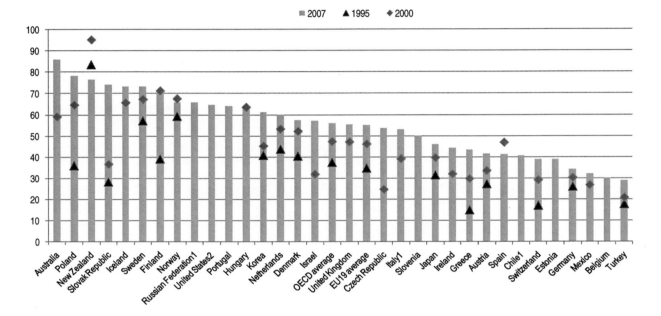

1. The entry rates for tertiary-type A programmes are calculated on a gross basis.

2. The entry rates for tertiary-type A programmes include the entry rates for tertiary-type B programmes.

Source: OECD (2009), *Education at a Glance*, OECD, Paris.

This growing receptivity is closely linked to the diversification of educational profiles observed in recent years. The steady growth in the ranks of students from a lower socio-economic background challenges tertiary education institutions to deal with a population that is less ready to make academic and professional choices, more exposed to the risk of failure, and more likely to drop out (Selz and Vallet, 2006; Galland and Rouault, 1996). Greater international mobility has also increased the proportion of foreign students in tertiary education institutions, which must now deal with the expectations and specific needs of students who are less at ease linguistically (OECD, 2004, 2005). The spread of vocational training and lifelong learning has also boosted the numbers of older students returning to tertiary education to follow courses related to their job or compatible with their previous experience (Douglas, 2004).

This growing receptivity also reflects the impact of policies developed since the early 1990s to promote inclusion of persons with disabilities at all levels of the education system, as a result of which a growing number of young adults with disabilities who wish to enrol in tertiary education can hope to do so (OECD, 1999, 2003).

**Figure 2.3. Students receiving additional resources during compulsory education
for a disability (CNC A) (1999-2003)**

As a percentage of all students

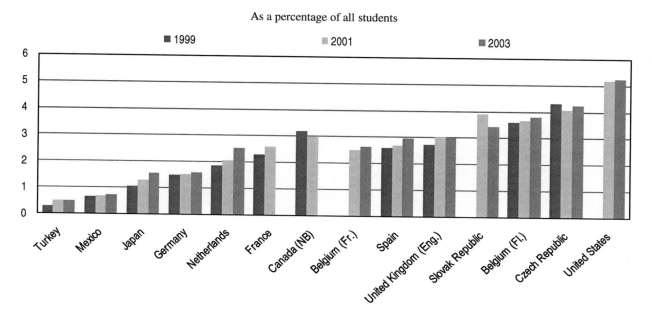

Source: OECD (2007), *Students with Disabilities, Learning Difficulties and Disadvantages: Policies, Statistics and Indicators*. OECD, Paris.

**Figure 2.4. Students receiving additional resources during compulsory education
for a specific learning difficulty (CNC B) (1999-2003)**

As a percentage of all students

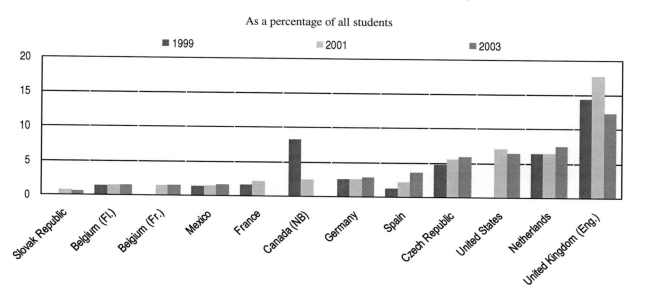

Source: OECD (2007), *Students with Disabilities, Learning Difficulties and Disadvantages: Policies, Statistics and Indicators*, OECD, Paris.

As Figure 2.3 shows, the proportion of students receiving additional resources for a disability or illness has risen in many OECD countries, especially in the Czech Republic and in the United States. Figure 2.4 indicates that the proportion of students receiving additional resources for a specific learning difficulty also rose in the Czech Republic and in France between 1999 and 2003, but not in the United States.

Mobilise financial means to promote inclusion

Inclusion policies have required significant supplementary funding, in addition to that provided by the health-care and social protection systems, in order to make the education system pedagogically and socially more accessible. Information from countries on the funding provided to implement these policies differs in quality and in importance. However, few countries have reliable statistics on the impact of policies for students with disabilities and are able to identify their cost-effectiveness.

Nevertheless, the country reports reveal the growing share of resources dedicated to mainstream education of children with disabilities. The United States has increased the federal share of funding for special education by 3.1% since 2008, to the equivalent of EUR 8 billion. The portion earmarked for covering the extra costs associated with disability in the regular school system rose by 3% between 2001 and 2009 to the equivalent of EUR 1 230 per child. In 2009, the Education Department devoted 11.5% (EUR 8.3 billion) of the FY 2010 budget under the *American Recovery and Reinvestment Act* (ARRA) to the education of students with disabilities within the framework of the *Individuals with Disabilities Act* (IDEA), Part B (611), and 0.5% (EUR 96 million) to the vocational rehabilitation of individuals with disabilities (*Fiscal Year 2010 Budget Summary*; US Department of Education, 2010).

In France, disability-related spending as a proportion of GDP rose from 1.75% in 2000 to 1.91% in 2006, when education-targeted spending accounted for around 0.39% of GDP. Funding for the education of students with disabilities was boosted substantially by the *Law on equal rights and opportunities for participation and citizenship for persons with disabilities* of 11 February 2005 to nearly EUR 260 million. For example, the bureau for school education (*mission de l'enseignement scolaire*) devoted EUR 197 million in 2009 to recruiting teachers' assistants to act with children enrolled in mainstream classes on a one-to-one basis (up by 30% over 2008) and EUR 42.6 million for teachers' assistants in special classes (up by 11% over 2008). In addition, EUR 13 million was earmarked for adapted teaching materials, and EUR 300 000 to support tertiary education students with disabilities in preparatory classes for the *grandes écoles*, as well as in advanced engineering sections. France also decided to create 2 000 special classes at the upper secondary level (*unités pédagogiques individualisées*) by 2010 (Délégation ministérielle à l'emploi des personnes handicapées, 2009).

In Ireland, spending on the schooling of students with disabilities in primary and secondary education rose by 28% between 2006 and 2008 to EUR 900 million while the budget for students with disabilities doubled between 2003 and 2008 to EUR 11.7 million. This budget served to triple the number of teachers' assistants between 1997 and 2006, bringing the total to 10 000; it quadrupled the number of resource teachers between 1998 and 2008 and raised the number of teachers working with students with disabilities by 300%. Sums allocated to the Fund for Students with Disabilities have increased by 42% since 2005, to EUR 2 953 per student, with amounts varying depending on the type of impairment. In the further education sector, allocations in 2007-08 averaged EUR 19 000 per student with a hearing impairment, EUR 16 000 per student with multiple disabilities, EUR 14 000 per student with a visual impairment, EUR 10 000 per student with an autistic disorder, EUR 3 500 per student with a learning difficulty, and EUR 2 000 per student with a psychological disorder (Higher Education Authority, 2009).

Very little information is available on funding for educating children with disabilities in other countries participating in the project. Norway could not identify resources specifically devoted to their education and training; these amounts are included in the lump-sum allocations to municipalities and counties based on their demographic profile and are not identifiable as such. The report indicates, however, that spending on the national system of special education amounted to nearly EUR 77 million in 2009 and funding to private institutions for the education of students with disabilities stood at EUR 18 million, while EUR 1 million went to training centres enrolling apprentices with disabilities.

Denmark provided no data on financing for the education of children and young adults with disabilities. Its report noted however that the budget for support to students with disabilities in tertiary education rose by 23% between 2004 and 2006 to EUR 6 million. In 2006, the handicap supplement amounted to EUR 7.3 million.

Promoting equity: a responsibility of educational institutions

An educational approach to disability

The growing number of students with disabilities in tertiary education reflects initiatives to make the education system more equitable and to allow every individual's active participation in facilitating social and professional inclusion. The equity requirement reflects a gradual shift away from the diagnostic approach to disability, which emphasises what children with disabilities and young adults cannot achieve, in favour of an educational perspective which relates disability to the capacity of the education system to place every student, regardless of his or her particular circumstances, on an equal footing in terms of access, outcomes and prospects (UNESCO, 1994; WHO, 2001; UN, 2006). In Ireland, the definition of disability in the *Education for Persons with Special Education Needs Act* emphasises the means to be mobilised to allow a person with a disability or a specific learning difficulty to exercise his or her legally recognised right to education; the *Disability Act* of 2005 requires secondary and tertiary education institutions to ensure that meeting students' educational needs is an integral component of their activity. In Norway, the 2001 White Paper entitled *From User to Citizen* considers disability in terms of the barriers that make it difficult for persons with disabilities to access education and employment and thus hinder their full participation; it gives priority to ensuring accessibility rather than focusing on impairment. The Danish agency responsible for allocating support to tertiary education students with disabilities considers disability a functional or psychological limitation that temporarily or permanently denies children and young adults equal opportunities of access to and success in secondary or tertiary education.

France's law of 11 February 2005 adopted a definition of disability: "a disability is any limitation on activity or restriction on participation in social life that a person suffers in his or her environment because of a substantial, lasting or definitive damage in one or more physical, sensory, mental, cognitive or psychological functions, a multiple disability, or a long-term health problem". The Czech Republic, where inclusion policies are even more recent, retains a diagnostic approach, which considers disability as a physical, mental, visual, auditory or multiple impairment, a language problem, an autistic disorder, a specific learning difficulty or a behavioural difficulty. In this way it refers the learning difficulties that students with disabilities may have to a medical condition, a long-term illness, or a minor impairment that hinders behavioural or learning capacities and must be taken into consideration from the educational point of view.

These differences affect the profiles of tertiary education students who are considered disabled. Countries in which the diagnostic approach of disability prevails (or which, like France, have moved beyond that approach only recently) mainly identify students with an impairment (motor or sensory) as having a disability. Countries that have adopted an educational approach to disability link it instead to the inaccessibility of the education system and identify for the most part as disabled those students with a specific learning disability.

Accessibility, a requirement for equity

The equity requirement means that the education system must adapt to the diversity of educational profiles and be pedagogically, physically, socially and psychologically accessible. In Denmark, schools must ensure that students with disabilities enjoy equal opportunities and treatment, and the Ministry of Education must provide the compensatory aids which a person with a disability needs in order to be able to follow the same courses as peers without disabilities and succeed academically. In France, schools are required to take positive measures for students with disabilities and to adapt academic pathways physically as well as pedagogically. In Ireland and Norway, schools must make arrangements to reduce as far as possible the impact of disability on a student's academic performance, and each tertiary education institution is expected to have a service that deals with disability issues. In the United States, the *Americans with Disabilities Act* (ADA) of 1990 prohibits discrimination on the basis of disability and requires schools to provide reasonable accommodations or auxiliary aids and services to qualified individuals with disabilities. In Norway, schools must ensure that students with disabilities have the same chances of success as other students. In the Czech Republic, every school is required to have a pedagogical and career guidance counsellor, to provide the necessary teaching and technical aids, and to support students throughout their school career.

The accessibility requirement does not take the same form in tertiary education as in secondary education. They are usually under a legal obligation to make appropriate arrangements for persons with educational needs resulting from a disability or a specific learning difficulty which has been medically or psychologically certified. Nevertheless, they are expected to create an educational environment that will facilitate success for all students, particularly the most vulnerable. In many countries, they are asked to make disability issues part of their institutional policy and to prepare action plans backed by operational provisions and establish the services to implement them. In Norway, tertiary education institutions are required to observe standards of universal accessibility and to establish co-ordination units in which representatives of students with and without disabilities, ministries and the university can discuss disability issues three or four times a year. In the United States, universities must make reasonable accommodation for students with disabilities. In Denmark, they are expected to ensure physical accessibility and to adapt the course of study to the needs of students with disabilities so that they receive the same education as the general population. They must take steps to identify the educational needs of students indicating a disability or a specific learning problem at the beginning of the academic year, after which they must apply for funds from the authorities responsible for financing support and make the necessary arrangements in terms of examinations, teaching aids and technical support. In Ireland, as in Denmark, it is up to the university, as part of its responsibilities under the right to education, to submit an application on behalf of the student for financing from the Fund for Students with Disabilities: that application form includes a registration form, a document certifying the student's special education need or disability, and a statement of the assistance required.

The accessibility requirement takes different forms in different countries. In Norway and Denmark, accessibility is an integral part of the mission of schools and universities, which are required to be accessible to all students, including those with disabilities. These countries do not have legislation prohibiting discrimination or have only recently adopted an anti-discrimination law; in Norway, it came into force in 2009. This legislation associates lack of accessibility with a form of discrimination and requires schools as well as employers to make their premises accessible in accordance with universal design standards. Danish legislation does not formally prohibit discrimination against persons with disabilities except for employment. However, it effectively bans discrimination in education by stipulating that students with disabilities must have the same opportunities as others for success. In this respect, transition to tertiary education depends on the ability of the education system to consider the diversity of educational profiles without ignoring the specific characteristics of children and young adults who have a disability, a long-term illness or a specific learning difficulty.

These countries differ from Ireland, France and the United States, which have adopted legislation prohibiting all forms of discrimination based on disability and requiring institutions to take steps to give equal opportunities to upper secondary school students and young adults with disabilities. The French *Law on equal rights and opportunities, participation and citizenship for persons with disabilities* of 11 February 2005 requires schools to enrol any person with a disability or a long-term health problem residing in their catchment area and to take positive measures on that person's behalf. Irish law treats as discrimination any refusal or inability to make reasonable accommodation for the needs of persons with disabilities. American legislation is stricter, especially for schools. The *Individuals with Disabilities Education Act* (IDEA) requires schools to ensure that students with a disability are on an equal footing in terms of access and academic success, while the *Americans with Disabilities Act* (ADA) of 1990 requires tertiary education institutions to make the necessary arrangements for accessibility at no cost to the student.

In this respect, these countries differ from the Czech Republic, which does not have very stringent anti-discrimination legislation. While the education law guarantees equal opportunity in education and prohibits any form of discrimination on grounds of health, the requirement applies only to public institutions of higher education. Moreover, a school director or principal may legally refuse to admit a child with a disability, but the decision must be justified.

These differences can affect the chances of young adults with disabilities to enter tertiary education. Their chances are greater in countries with laws that prohibit any form of discrimination because of a health problem or a disability and that oblige educational institutions to offer all students equal opportunities for success, than in countries where such legislation is weak or non-existent. In the Czech Republic, for example, students with disabilities enrolled in ISCED 5B tertiary education represent only 0.08% of the student body in that stream, while in the United States 11% of such students declared a disability (Horn and Nevill, 2006).

Anti-discrimination laws make secondary and tertiary education institutions responsible for including the diversity of educational needs in their mission, developing a strategy within their action plan, and offering, under more or less clearly defined conditions, the human, technical and financial resources needed to make them accessible to all students. By requiring schools to enrol all applicants presenting a disability, a specific learning difficulty or a long-term illness, the French *Law on equal rights and opportunities, participation and citizenship of persons with disabilities* of 11 February 2005 has done much to strengthen their chances of access to education. The proportion of students with disabilities enrolled in lower and upper secondary education rose for example by 18% between 2006 and 2007. These anti-discrimination laws also prevent students with disabilities from being caught up in the diversity issue (ministère de l'Éducation nationale and ministère de l'Enseignement supérieur et de la Recherche, 2010). Danish and Norwegian student services do not always pay sufficient attention to students with disabilities as part of their concerns, and may thus deny them the support available to the population as a whole.

Empower high school students and high schools to ensure inclusion

The growing numbers of students with disabilities in tertiary education also reflect the technical, human and financial resources that countries have devoted to enabling secondary and tertiary education institutions to meet the demand for accessibility and to support young adults with disabilities in satisfying academic, social and professional requirements.

Give students with disabilities equal opportunities to succeed

The growing number of students with disabilities enrolled in tertiary education is closely related to the additional resources for ensuring that they have equal opportunities for access and success. Allocation of these resources depends on the learning needs identified during the pedagogical and psychological assessments conducted by the institutions or by specialised teams. They are supposed to be formalised in an individual education plan (IEP) which establishes the objectives pursued, the means allocated and the methods of evaluation.

These resources may be used to facilitate access to course content. In Ireland, they take the form of technical aids provided by the schools, transport and summer programmes. They also cover 84 education assistants for Roma students (nearly half of them), and support students with a hearing impairment (a third of them) and a visual impairment (16% of them). In Denmark, students with disabilities receive support in the form of a sign language or LPC[1] interpreter, while in France 8.4% of students with disabilities enrolled in mainstream education in 2006 had the services of a teacher's assistant, and 8% received adapted learning materials.

These resources also take the form of pedagogical arrangements to facilitate academic progress and success. These include a possible extension of the course of study. In the United States, for example, high school students with a disability can remain in secondary schooling through the age of 21. In Norway, upper secondary students with disabilities may extend the course by two years if included in their IEP. In France, examination candidates may be allowed to carry their marks over from one year to the next and spread

---

1. The LPC method (also named verbo-tonal method) is a technique associating movements of the hands and lips.

the tests over several sessions. These arrangements can also relate, as in Denmark, to the number of subjects studied, the timetable, or teaching practices.

Special examination arrangements are another form of support granted to upper secondary school students with disabilities. In Ireland, students with disabilities enrolled in upper secondary education are entitled to special arrangements in certificate examinations such as sign language interpreters, readers, scribes, adaptation of the format of questions, use of Braille, tape recorders and adaptive technology as well as exemptions. According to the country report, 54% of students with disabilities who prepared the leaving certificate in 2007 and 58% of those working for the applied leaving certificate were exempted from tests or were given spelling and grammar exemptions (Higher Education Authority, 2009). In addition, 27.9% of students and 30.8% of those preparing for the applied leaving certificate received reading support. According to the National Longitudinal Transition Study (NLTS2) in the United States, among students with disabilities who received assistance because of their disability, 68% of those benefiting from special arrangements, support and services had additional time to complete tests. In addition, the testing methods differed for 9% and 5% had different tests (Newman *et al.*, 2009).

Information on modes of funding provided in the reports varies in its scope and quality. However, the financing of these resources differs by country and destination. Support for secondary school students with disabilities may be funded from the institution's budget for legally required pedagogical accessibility, as in the United States. It may also be covered by funds specifically earmarked for the student's identified learning need in addition to the institution's budget. In Denmark, funding comes from the Danish educational support agency (*Styrelsen for Statens Uddannelsesstøtte*), which falls under the responsibility of the Ministry of Education. In Norway, additional resources allocated to schools are proportionate to the number of students with special needs education. In France, pedagogical adaptations are financed by the local education authorities (*rectorats*) following procedures set out in the student's personalised academic programme and subject to validation by the Commission on the Rights and Autonomy of Persons with Disabilities (*Commission des droits et de l'autonomie des personnes handicapées* – CDAPH) on the recommendation of the Departmental Offices for Persons with Disabilities (MDPH).

This support may also be correlated, as in Ireland, with the institutional profile, the number of students with disabilities enrolled, the type of disabilities and their degree of severity. For students with a "low-incidence disability", schools benefit from a weekly "resource teaching" time allowance, depending on the type of disability. Four hours are allotted for students with a sensory impairment, three hours for those with a motor deficiency, and five hours for an autistic disorder or a severe specific learning disability.

When students have a high-incidence disability, schools allot 90 minutes of supplementary instruction, thereby ensuring a minimum of 2.5 hours of instruction in subgroups of students with the same support needs. Secondary schools with fewer than 600 students are provided with teaching support hours equivalent to 0.7 of a full-time teacher each week to meet the needs of students with difficulties in reading or maths, while those with a larger student body are eligible for teaching hours equivalent to 1.2 full-time teacher.

Mobilise schools to focus on the diversity of educational profiles

The growing proportion of upper secondary school students with disabilities applying for tertiary education is also attributable to the methodological support offered to institutions. In Norway, guidance services financed by the counties help to prevent dropouts, while the psycho-educational support services help to diversify pedagogical organisation and to differentiate teaching practices (Figure 2.5). The national special education support system, the specialised diagnostic centres, and the government-run councils co-ordinated by the education and training directorate provide support to the schools in assessing needs, in preparing the IEP, in adapting pedagogical practices and differentiating pedagogical organisation, and in co-ordinating support to students. In France, the Special Education and Home Care Services (SESSAD) provide support for students with disabilities, offering advice on specific aspects of their impairment and its pedagogical implications, making other children and parents aware of the importance of welcoming a child with disabilities, and thus making it easier for teachers, other children and parents to accept them. The academic authorities have instituted networks of "resource teachers" to counsel, assist and support teachers in upper secondary education. In Denmark special funding is available to schools for their assessment activities, pedagogical innovations, and research and dissemination of studies.

Figure 2.5. Support services provided to secondary schools enrolling students with disabilities in Norway

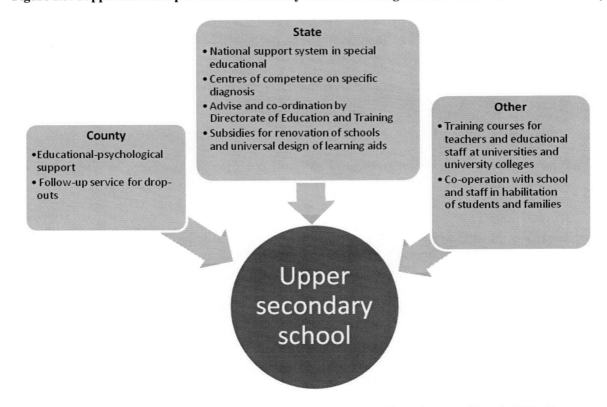

Source: Legard, S. (2009), "Pathways from Education to Work for Young People with Impairments and Learning Difficulties in Norway", Work Research Institute, Oslo.

Training for teachers and principals is another form of support to schools. In Ireland, more than 15 000 teachers received professional training in 2007 from the Special Education Support Service. France has improved teacher training and made pedagogical and digital resources available. It has also created a training course for upper secondary school teachers and principals to help them work with students with disabilities.

Owing to the lack of statistics it is not possible to assess fully the impact of these resources on secondary school students with disabilities. However, joint action targeted at young adults with disabilities and schools is an important factor in opening institutions to diversity and in the empowerment of students and their families (OECD, 1999). Additional resources, particularly financial resources or resources for meeting examination requirements, are considered essential to their academic success by 40% of high school students with disabilities in Norway and by a majority of American students (Bjerkan and Veenstra, 2008; Newman *et al.*, 2009). In France, for example, the number of students with disabilities enrolled in upper secondary education rose by 10% between 2005 and 2007, and it quadrupled in the Czech Republic between 2006 and 2008 (ministère de l'Éducation nationale and ministère de l'Enseignement supérieur et de la Recherche, 2010; Ministry of Education of the Czech Republic, 2009). As Figure 2.6 shows, the proportion of students with disabilities enrolled in regular classes and receiving additional resources for a disability increased between 1999 and 2003 in most OECD countries.

Figure 2.6. Students receiving additional resources for disability or illness, by type of schooling (CNC A) (2003)

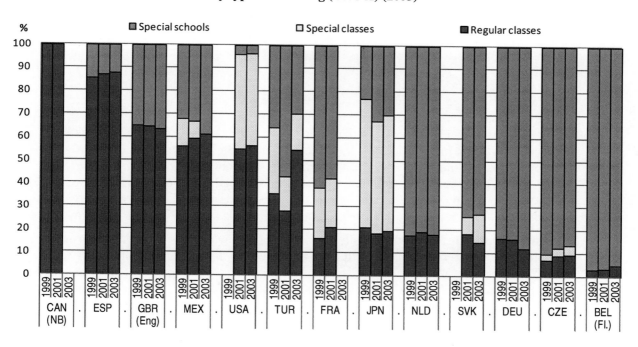

Source: OECD (2007), *Students with Disabilities, Learning Difficulties and Disadvantages: Policies, Statistics and Indicators*, OECD, Paris.

In Ireland, 5 934 secondary school students requested pedagogical support in 2008, and 1 220 asked for the help of a special needs assistant. Students seeking pedagogical support in secondary school most often had a severe learning difficulty (24%), an emotional or behavioural disorder (14%), a moderate learning difficulty (13%), a slight learning difficulty (13%), a physical impairment (10%), or autism (8%). This distribution contrasts with that of students requesting the help of a special needs teacher, who most frequently had an emotional or behavioural disorder (21%), a mobility impairment (18%), autism (16%), or a slight learning difficulty (16%) (Higher Education Authority, 2009).

Mobilisation of tertiary education institutions and their students

Help students with disabilities to succeed in tertiary education

Generally speaking, students with disabilities in tertiary education are entitled to the same kinds of support as in secondary education. They have the right to technical and human aids provided by the bodies in charge of compensating for disability. It is the responsibility of the institution to provide them, as necessary, with mimeographs or photocopies of targeted courses and studies, tape recordings and transcriptions, or Braille documents, to lend them specialised materials or to provide them with tutors or note takers. In Ireland, the Fund for Students with Disabilities pays for adapted learning materials (computers, printers, scanners, dictaphones), human assistance (personal assistant, note taker, educational support, specific courses) and transport costs: 3 099 students received a total of more than EUR 13 million in 2007-08, up by 52% from 2005 (Higher Education Authority, 2009). Danish young adults eligible for special education support (SPS) are entitled to assistance and counselling in respect of needs assessment, technological aids, interpreters and note takers.

Norway uses financial incentives to encourage tertiary education institutions to provide alternative forms of examination and assessment and to step up monitoring during the course of study. It also asks them to have a disability support service specifically dedicated to students with disabilities, to provide them with the technical and pedagogical aids needed for their course of study and to make special examination arrangements. In countries where universities apply admissions tests, young adults with disabilities may ask for special arrangements: interviews during the site visit in the Czech Republic revealed that in 2008, 302 students with disabilities enrolled in the Mazaryk University of Brno benefited from technical aids and special forms of communication for their entrance exams, and 10% of these had taken preparatory sessions offered by the disability support service before the tests.

On the financial front, young adults with disabilities have access to the same financial support as the general student body. In Norway, they may, like other students, apply for a state-funded study loan or bursary (*statens lanekasse*), with the loan partially changed into a bursary if they pass their examinations. In the United States, full-time students can apply for bursaries, non-repayable grants, loans or state or federally funded allowances managed by the university. According the country report, the Federal Pell Grant awards funding to undergraduate students and distributed nearly EUR 15 million in 2009, and the Federal Stafford Loan for undergraduate and graduate students gears the amount to the student's financial need. The loan is repaid at variable rates, with the federal government picking up the interest cost under exceptional circumstances. Students with disabilities may also apply for the allowances and loans offered by most states. For example, the Bank of America scholarship is awarded by the Learning Disabilities Associations of Arkansas and Iowa to high school seniors who plan a career in finance, commerce or computer sciences, and a scholarship is offered by the National Center for Learning Disabilities to high school graduates with a specific learning difficulty whose qualities and conduct may serve as models to other young adults with disabilities. Young adults with disabilities may also be eligible for university-sponsored scholarships such as those offered by George Washington University in Washington, DC; these scholarships range from EUR 700 to EUR 7 000 and are awarded to 15 students with disabilities whose registration costs are paid by the vocational rehabilitation sector.

Young adults with disabilities are also entitled to funding to offset the extra costs of living with a disability or a specific learning difficulty. In Denmark, the "handicap supplement" compensates young adults eligible for the special education allowance for the loss of income linked to difficulties in accessing employment during university studies. In Norway, students with disabilities may extend their course of study by one year without jeopardising their loans or bursaries; if they are obliged to break off their studies, temporarily or not, for health reasons, their loan can be converted into a grant. Studies conducted in Norway indicate that 30% of students finance their studies with funding provided by the National Insurance Scheme by holding part-time jobs or through other arrangements (Bjerkan and Veenstra, 2008) (Figure 2.7). In France, bursaries available to students with disabilities are increased for a permanent disability or a mental health problem requiring permanent assistance by another person. Bursaries are not bound by an age limit for students whose disability is documented by the Commission for the rights and the autonomy of persons with disabilities (*Commission des droits et de l'autonomie des personnes handicapées* – CDAPH); they can be combined with the financial resources received for their disability. Students with slight psychological disorders, a mobility impairment, or a visual, auditory or mental health problem, permanent or temporary, may apply for special bursaries on the recommendation of the Commission on the autonomy of persons with disabilities (*Commission des droits et de l'autonomie des personnes handicapées*). The award of a bursary exempts the recipient from registration fees.

Encourage universities to include disability issues in their institutional policy

The growing proportion of students with disabilities enrolled in tertiary education is closely linked to the resources provided to institutions (OECD, 2003). These resources may take the form of financial incentives designed to offset the additional costs that the presence of a student with special education needs may represent for the institution. Ireland devotes 1% of the annual tertiary education budget to accommodating disadvantaged groups (including students with disabilities), while the Higher Education Authority allocates EUR 42.50 an hour for additional learning support and has adopted a per capita financing formula for certain categories of disabilities to improve efficiency and enhance strategic use of the available resources in institutions. In 2009 the United States devoted 1.3% of its budget for persons with disabilities (transition, technical assistance, research, staff preparedness, services to persons with disabilities or financial assistance) to projects designed to support tertiary education. According to information provided by the report, in 2010, 78% of this budget went towards financing scholarships or loans which universities may allocate to the neediest students. In France, tertiary education institutions are given an annual budgetary envelope calculated in light of the costs of support and arrangements provided to students with disabilities.

Figure 2.7. Types of support to students with disabilities enrolled in tertiary education in Norway

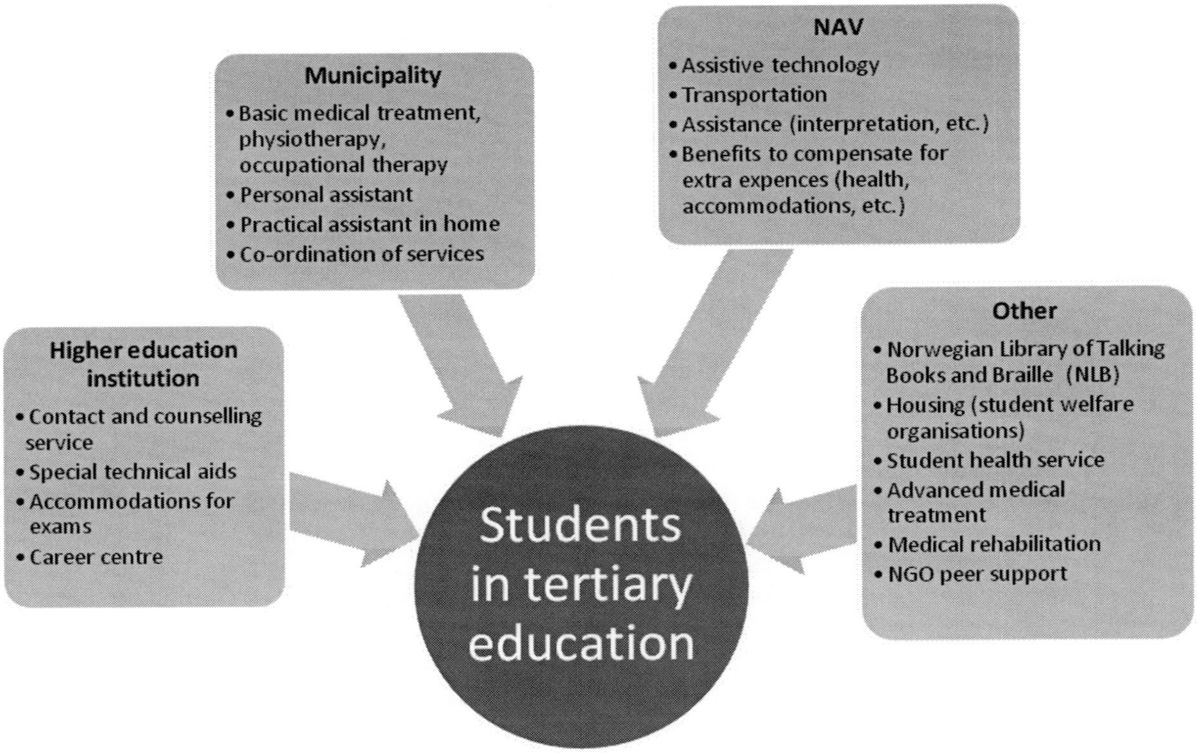

Municipality
- Basic medical treatment, physiotherapy, occupational therapy
- Personal assistant
- Practical assistant in home
- Co-ordination of services

NAV
- Assistive technology
- Transportation
- Assistance (interpretation, etc.)
- Benefits to compensate for extra expences (health, accommodations, etc.)

Higher education institution
- Contact and counselling service
- Special technical aids
- Accommodations for exams
- Career centre

Other
- Norwegian Library of Talking Books and Braille (NLB)
- Housing (student welfare organisations)
- Student health service
- Advanced medical treatment
- Medical rehabilitation
- NGO peer support

Students in tertiary education

Source: Legard, S. (2009), "Pathways from Education to Work for Young People with Impairments and Learning Difficulties in Norway", Work Research Institute, Oslo.

Financial incentives may also seek to support pedagogical innovation, skills upgrading of institutional staff or research into tertiary education and training for young adults with disabilities in tertiary education. The US Department of Education supports model demonstration projects to ensure that students with disabilities receive a tertiary education experience of high quality. Grantees must develop effective teaching methods to enhance the skills and abilities of postsecondary faculty working with students with disabilities. Ireland's New Strategic Innovation Fund, created in 2006, finances projects that support an education policy to improve the quality of instruction and the academic level of students and to promote lifelong learning.

The incentives may also be methodological in nature. France encourages staff responsible for the admission and support of students with disabilities enrolled in tertiary education to share their practices and experience through networking; less frequently, it offers specific training courses. The United States has created a federal technical centre within the Department of Education to support efforts to improve the enrolment rate of students with disabilities in tertiary education, and it is planning to offer tools to universities in the form of good practice manuals identifying ways and means of improving the quality of admission and support. In addition, the Tertiary Education Commission of New Jersey administers a budget of USD 1.6 billion (EUR 1.2 billion) for the Special Needs Grant Programme, which is allocated to the regional centres that support the state's tertiary education institutions and their students. Norway has created a resource centre based in Trondheim to inform young adults with disabilities about the degree of accessibility of institutions and to advise universities on matters such as universal design, teaching aids and special examination arrangements. In Ireland, the Disability Advisors Working Network (DAWN) provides admissions and support staff help in exchanging information on problems and solutions. This network of advisors has drawn up a guide for university personnel to raise their awareness of disability issues and encourage them to take account of the diversity of student profiles.

These financial and methodological incentives have made universities more receptive to the diversity of educational profiles. In Ireland, the number of students with disabilities in tertiary education deemed eligible for support nearly doubled between 2005 and 2008, and spending rose by 42% to EUR 11.6 million. The number of young adults enrolled in further education courses benefiting from the Fund for Students with Disabilities quadrupled between 2003 and 2008 to 401 individuals, for an amount of more than EUR 3 million, *i.e.* a 400% increase (Higher Education Authority, 2009). The site visit revealed that the number of services provided to students with disabilities at Trinity College Dublin rose by 70% between 2006 and 2008, and involved primarily adaptation of books (28.9%), photocopy (25.4%), and training in the use of technical aids (13.1%).

In the United States, the number of tertiary education institutions accepting students with disabilities has risen by 90% since 1990 (National Center on Secondary Education and Transition, 2000). According to the NLTS2 survey, in addition to the special examination arrangements described earlier, young adults with disabilities enrolled in tertiary education were granted tutors (31.0%), note takers (26.0%), technology aids (11.8%), readers or interpreters (10.1%), learning/behaviour management support (10.1%), early registration (6.6%), independent living support (3.9%), physical adaptations to classroom (3.1%), and books in Braille (Newman *et al.*, 2009). The country report from Denmark shows that the number of special education support beneficiaries rose from 0.5% to 0.7% of the total student population between 2004 and 2006; funds were allocated for interpretation services (30.6%), study support hours (19.1%), digital support services (16.7%), teaching materials (15.1%), support tools and instruction on their use (6.1%), educational needs assessment (5.3%), special workspace accommodation (1.7%) and courses (1.1%).

These initiatives have led tertiary education institutions to make disability a component of their institutional strategy, but with varying degrees of openness and commitment. In France, universities and the *grandes écoles* have signed a charter with the government which commits them to develop the individual and collective means needed to ensure equal opportunities for students with disabilities. The body of university presidents (*Conférence des Presidents d'Université*) and that of the *grandes écoles* (*Conférence des grandes écoles*) aim at improving the admission opportunities of young adults with disabilities. Some universities visited during the project, such as Trinity College Dublin, have adopted and implemented a policy of support for the entire university community and draw attention to initiatives to include disadvantaged students, including those with a disability or a learning difficulty. Other institutions raise awareness of the disability issue within the university community by asking each faculty to appoint a person responsible for assisting students with disabilities, for seeing that support and others arrangements are properly applied, and for maintaining links with colleagues, the administration and other students. Masaryk University in Brno has endeavoured to create a pedagogical environment accessible to students with disabilities, with an electronic study agenda, 55 specially equipped workstations with computer aids in laboratories and lecture rooms, personal assistants, tutors, note takers and sign language interpreters. It has also developed a library with more than 1 000 volumes in Braille for students with a visual impairment.

Tertiary education institutions have also been developing special services for the admission and counselling of students with disabilities, so as to ensure a pedagogical environment that fosters their success and respects their rights (for Denmark, see Box 2.1). The University of Paris 8 has considerably expanded and upgraded the qualifications of the team working in its student disability support services, created in 2003, which define and implement admissions strategies. Personnel interviewed during the visit said they help candidates to fulfil administrative requirements, counsel them as necessary and carry out, when necessary, required administrative procedures. They also arrange for the necessary study aids and support: to this end they assess educational needs, identify the support required, mobilise the necessary personnel, and contact the teaching staff to ensure implementation.

Box 2.1. Guidance and support at Aarhus University, Denmark

The Counselling and Support Centre offers guidance and support to postsecondary students with a disability as well as those whose mother tongue is not Danish.

Its main responsibilities include:

1. Counselling and support services:
   a) counselling and support for students encountering particular difficulties in their studies;
   b) counselling and support in applying for aid.

2. Supply of special pedagogical support to students:
   a) to apply for financing;
   b) to implement supplemental measures;
   c) general counselling and advice for students at the university and in other tertiary education institutions in Denmark;
   d) guidance for persons responsible for special pedagogical support in other institutions in Denmark.

3. Research and development:
   a) development of special counselling and support practices;
   b) research in specific fields based on the centre's practice, such as counselling, dyslexia, inclusion of students in educational institutions and the labour market.

4. Creation of a skilled national guidance centre in adapted pedagogy:
   a) establishment of a national pedagogical research and development centre to develop methods, gather experience and communicate knowledge on pedagogy adapted to the secondary and postsecondary school curricula in Denmark.

Source: Counselling and Support Centre, Aarhus University

These services also work closely with teachers who may need information or support in order to adapt their practice to the needs of students with disabilities. They may also pursue specific action with target groups such as students with mental health problems. For example, the disability support service of Trinity College Dublin devoted 46% of its time in 2008 to assisting students with disabilities, 28% of its time to administrative tasks, 13% to defining and implementing projects, and 8% to computer technologies. It spent much less time at meetings outside the university (4%) and on staff training (1%).

In some countries, universities have developed special training courses for students with disabilities. In Ireland, Trinity College Dublin, in collaboration with University College Cork, has developed a certificate for students with an intellectual impairment, offering instruction in the plastic arts, applied arts and professional development. The Technology Institute Tallaght, in collaboration with the technology institutes of Blanchardstown, Carlow and Dun Laoghaire, has created a collaborative network for innovation in education and inclusive education focused on various aspects of inclusive education (learner and staff support, learning styles, problem-based learning, emotional competences, technical aids). In the United States, many tertiary education institutions have developed teaching programmes specifically geared to students with disabilities. Some specialise in a specific type of impairment, while others are more generic. When they are exclusively devoted to students with severe cognitive, intellectual or developmental problems, these programmes may teach behavioural skills and offer experience in selected jobs and functions (meal preparation) without conferring course credits. Other teaching programmes help young adults with disabilities to make contact with other students and to acquire work experience on or off campus. Still others include personalised support services (coaching, technical aids) so that the students can attend the same classes as others.

Adelphi University, for example, has a programme for young adults with specific learning difficulties designed to encourage their independence, assist them in realising their academic potential, and help dismantle barriers to their social and professional inclusion. The University of Arizona's Strategic Alternatives Learning Techniques Centre offers support to 550 postsecondary students with learning difficulties or attention deficit disorders for personalised learning strategies, educational planning, tutoring and technical aids. Institutions such as George Washington University offer remedial courses and help in finding a tutor.

Promote an education system that focuses on every student's success

Ensure transitions adapted to the diversity of students' educational needs

Beyond specific initiatives on their behalf, the growing number of students with disabilities enrolled in tertiary education can be attributed to the promotion of an education system that creates educational environments that are sufficiently flexible to adapt to the diversity of educational needs. Educating students with disabilities in secondary and tertiary education is an integral part of education reforms to promote equality of treatment for all students. Ireland recognises that most schools have students with special educational needs, and that an appropriate response will facilitate their success. The principles of equality and inclusion are at the core of Norway's reform of its education system. Reform 94 sought explicitly to facilitate access for students with disabilities to upper secondary school, while Reform 97 introduced individualised learning plans in secondary school. The Knowledge Promotion Reform encouraged schools to pay more attention to the diversity of educational needs. IDEA in the United States seeks to reduce dropout rates, improve academic outcomes, and enhance the cognitive and functional aptitudes of students with disabilities by encouraging collaboration among stakeholders and services in a school or district.

To achieve this, schools are encouraged to have as their goal the success of each student, regardless of his or her circumstances, social origin or ethnic group. In the United States the 2001 *No Child Left Behind Act* requires education programmes to consider the potential and the prospects of every student, and to ensure that each student's knowledge is assessed (National Center on Secondary Education and Transition, 2004). The Danish government expects that at least 85% of youngsters in any age group, including students with disabilities, to have an upper secondary school diploma by 2010. In France, the education monitoring team must ensure that each student's course of study is geared to learning goals consistent with the prescribed curricular content. Ireland includes students with serious difficulties in reading and maths among those eligible for additional resources, in order to encourage schools not to overlook the weakest students. This is also one of the objectives of Norway's Knowledge Promotion Reform of 2006, in light of its PISA results, to induce schools to see themselves as learning organisations concerned with the success of each student, and to encourage tertiary education institutions to follow students more closely during their course of study and take measures (group work, less testing and written work) to improve their chances of success. In France, the *université/handicap* charter requires learning plans developed jointly by the institution and the student with disabilities to be both ambitious and realistic, based on concrete achievements consistent with the study path envisaged upon entry into tertiary education.

According to the reports, countries participating in the project were also committed to reducing absenteeism and the attendant risk of dropout to which upper secondary school students with disabilities are more exposed. Norway and Denmark have created monitoring services to ensure continuity into upper secondary school for the most vulnerable students (particularly those with impairments, behavioural problems or learning difficulties) and to avoid the risk of dropout. The Norwegian guidance services work with schools to encourage dropouts to return and complete secondary school. Danish high school students can, if they wish, receive weekly psychological counselling to help them overcome their difficulties or fears, and frequent absentees are called to the principal's office to discuss their situation. In the United States, the National Dropout Prevention Center for Students with Disabilities provides methodological support for building states' capacities to increase school completion rates.

Pedagogical flexibility also contributes to the success of every student, since the presence of students with disabilities is considered beneficial for the entire education system. Accessibility for all is generally based on establishing the conditions for the preparation, implementation and completion of an individual education plan. IDEA requires such plans to identify the ways in which the learning programmes will improve students' academic, developmental and functional aptitudes and facilitate the move to post-academic activities. As a way of increasing the success rate, Norway requires universities to establish an IEP for every student enrolled, whether or not that person has a special education need.

Excellence also requires secondary and tertiary education institutions to be accountable. Some countries have adopted a set of tools for tracking the performance of education systems. For example, in the United States IDEA obliges state education agencies to track the performance of their educational systems, and the Office of Special Education Programs (OSEP) uses indicators to monitor their performance. Indicator No. 1 is the proportion of high school students with an IEP graduating with a regular diploma, while indicator No. 2 is the proportion of students with an IEP who have dropped out. School surveys have also been conducted to determine what students (including those with disabilities) have learned and the conditions under which students with disabilities pursue their studies, as well as the impact of practices on their academic progress and success. Norway requires schools to report annually to the Ministry of Education on initiatives to enhance their accessibility and to maximise students' chances of success. In France, the law of 11 February 2005 provides for the regular evaluation of legislative measures such as those for education and access to employment.

The promotion of a school for all that is concerned for the success of all students, regardless of their circumstances, has been decisive in increasing access to postsecondary education. It has allowed a growing number of students with disabilities to go on to tertiary education and has strengthened equality of opportunity and treatment for such students. One result of Norway's tracking services is that 50% of students who have dropped out eventually finish their secondary school programme, and its "quality reform" is widely recognised as having reduced the postsecondary failure rate substantially. In the United States, the proportion of students with disabilities dropping out of high school fell by 20% between 1993 and 2003, and the percentage of those earning a high school diploma jumped 43% between 1996 and 2005 to 57% of all high school graduates. The proportion of young adults with disabilities leaving high school with a certificate rose by 6% over the same period (NCES, 2008).

Mobilise the education system around students' prospects

With the exception of the Czech Republic, where the transition to tertiary education and employment is not a responsibility of the Ministry of Education, countries participating in the project have (more or less recently) tasked their education systems with linking the education process to students' future prospects, their centres of interest and aptitudes, and to the various skills and qualities needed for their social and economic inclusion.

Denmark makes transition a component of school policies and students are required to draw up a transition plan at the end of primary school, setting out the future they see for themselves and the shape it might take. To this end, they receive coaching and support throughout secondary school in preparation for choosing an activity upon graduation, in line with their centres of interest and their capabilities and in light of the available offer. This monitoring may be provided in the context of bridging programmes that combine coaching and instruction during the last years of upper secondary school to encourage students to pursue their studies after graduation or to earn qualifications recognised by the labour market. In the United States, the individual education plans prepared by schools must include elements relating to the student's future, as of age 16 or earlier, in a transition plan that specifies the student's centres of interest, educational objectives, and ways of achieving them, as well as the monitoring arrangements proposed by the school.

In Norway, schools must provide counselling to students (including those with a disability or a specific learning difficulty) regarding their educational and career choices. France has recently begun to encourage active guidance counselling for all upper secondary education students to help them make informed choices based on objective information about the content and prerequisites of the programmes they wish to enter, the occupations to which this learning may lead, and their career opportunities. Along the lines of the transition year programme established for students after completion of lower secondary education and before the start of upper secondary education, Ireland has established an experimental transition year unit, piloted by the Higher Education Authority together with the National Council for Curriculum and Assessment (NCCA). This year is meant to allow upper secondary school students to explore their university and career options in light of their centres of interest and their aptitudes and to identify available support and services to meet their particular needs if they have a disadvantaged background or a disability.

Schools therefore now have staff responsible for making students aware of their future prospects, and many have a staff guidance counsellor to advise students on the conditions of access to tertiary education and the career opportunities for which education programmes prepare them. In Norway, for example, selected teachers are asked, in addition to their teaching duties, to help students with disabilities to prepare their transition to tertiary education or employment, to make the necessary arrangements to enter tertiary education as early as possible, and to integrate the issue of transition into the individual education plan as of the third year of secondary school. In France, providing active guidance to students with disabilities is the responsibility of the head teachers, the teachers in charge of the IEP, and to a lesser extent the guidance counsellors, whose role is to encourage high school students (including those with disabilities) to identify as soon as possible the university courses that correspond to their centres of interest, relying where necessary on information provided by the guidebook for tertiary education students with disabilities prepared by the Ministry of Tertiary Education and Research, and to obtain information from those responsible for university education. In the United States, teachers are expected to support high school students with disabilities in preparing their IEP, to participate in related meetings and to see that the necessary conditions are in place for achieving the objectives defined by the student, together with the players involved in the process (Department of Public Instruction, Department of Workforce Development, Department of Health Services, 2009).

Upper secondary schools are also encouraged to become integrated into their environment and to make students aware of labour market and tertiary education requirements. These linkages may be formal, as in Denmark, where they take the form of education programmes with a component that specifies academic and professional requirements or programmes that combine general and professional instruction in working internships to make students aware of labour market demands. As with the secondary-postsecondary learning options (SPLOs) in the United States, these linkages may also take the form of education programmes that allow high school students to take university-level courses to prepare them for the requirements of tertiary education and even obtain course credits. These linkages may also take the form of networks, such as the Disabilities, Opportunities, Internetworking and Technology (DO-IT) programme at George Washington University to prepare high school students with disabilities for the demands of tertiary education and introduce them to the use of new technologies, the role played by peer support, and on-the-job learning. This programme provides young adults with disabilities with portable computers, software and technical aids which that they can use at home, at school or at work to network with their peers, members of their programme team and tutors. These linkages may also take the form, as in France, of meetings to exchange information during which secondary and postsecondary education personnel discuss their practices and, if necessary, find answers to problems encountered in the process of advancing to tertiary education.

Diversify educational opportunities

Mobilising the education system to deal with students' future prospects requires smoothing the way, for example by eliminating bureaucratic constraints that impede progress. In Ireland, for example, students in tertiary education may apply for support at any time during the academic year and thus deal with disabilities or learning difficulties that may arise.

Smoothing the path is also made possible by the existence of bridges between the different education sectors and levels in order to diversify students' opportunities. Norway has authorised the transformation of a professional certificate into a university entrance certificate, thereby creating a bridge between general and professional programmes; students who have pursued ISCED 3B or 3C courses for two years are allowed to take a year of supplementary education validated by the university. The United States has various bridges in the form of alternative training programmes, "second chance" or alternative educational facilities, and horizontal programmes that facilitate access to tertiary education. Many universities also offer catch-up courses for young adults who fail the entry tests or cannot meet the prerequisites, and community colleges try to link their programmes to those of universities, thereby facilitating university recognition of students' course credits. Danish education programmes include internships in enterprises in the final year of upper secondary school to familiarise students with the demands of the labour market and working relations and make them more employable; students receive a skills certificate detailing outcomes and highlighting students' acquired skills. France offers university students who have taken ISCED 5A courses the possibility to switch to ISCED 5B courses and promotes validation of experience to facilitate employees' access to tertiary education and thereby strengthen the linkages between the worlds of work and education. Ireland validates knowledge acquired in ISCED 4 training, in the workplace or the voluntary sector, through the Further Education and Training Award (FETAC).

Ireland has also built new bridges between education sectors and levels in recent years. Thanks to the back-to-education allowance, 1 078 individuals (or 17.6% of programme beneficiaries) who had previously received a pension or allowance for a disability or long-term illness were able to improve their employability by strengthening their qualifications, two-thirds of them through postsecondary training (Higher Education Authority, 2009). The National Framework of Qualifications, established in 2003, facilitates the mobility of young adults seeking to extend their ISCED 4 or 5B training through courses at the ISCED 5A level by recognising the skills acquired at each stage of their educational or working career. The further education sector offers vocational education and training courses that facilitate access to employment as well as remedial instruction in preparation for tertiary education. In 2007, 331 young adults with disabilities took advantage of these arrangements, an increase of 143% over 2003, when they represented 0.07% of beneficiaries under a programme offered by this sector (Higher Education Authority, 2009).

The path can also be smoothed by special procedures or exemptions for disadvantaged groups, including persons with disabilities. Norway has created a special procedure whereby young adults with disabilities who lack a secondary school diploma can access tertiary education, with the proviso that they obtain this diploma during the first semester of university studies. They are also eligible for a special admissions procedure that allows them to register earlier than other students so that the necessary accommodations can be made in advance. In the United States, the *Higher Education Opportunity Act* of 2008 encourages access to tertiary education and employment for disadvantaged youth (including young adults with disabilities) by fostering partnerships between institutions serving primarily disadvantaged students and tertiary education institutions, as well as players in the business world and the labour market. Ireland has created the Supplementary Admissions Program under which young adults with disabilities who do not fully fulfil admission requirements can have access to tertiary education; in 2006 135 individuals (or one-quarter of applicants) benefited from this provision. In France, the *handicap/grandes écoles* charter offers special treatment to young adults with disabilities and gives them access to the *grandes écoles*, while the *cordée de la réussite* (roughly "the lifeline to success") seeks to remove the psychological and cultural obstacles that make it difficult for young adults from a low socio-economic background or enrolled in schools located in disadvantaged or rural areas to undertake the lengthy courses of study offered by the most reputable tertiary education institutions, in particular the *grandes écoles*.

Anchor students' paths in integrated transition systems

Some countries supplement the efforts of education institutions with administrative services that are responsible for the co-ordination and coherence of the transition process. Ireland has entrusted part of this task to the Central Applications Office (CAO) which co-ordinates applications to tertiary education institutions. On their application form, students can indicate a disability which can make them eligible for the supplementary admission route if they meet the criteria. Once a student has indicated a disability, the appropriate institution is notified so that preparation for post-entry support can begin. Norway has entrusted this task to the University Admissions Service (*Samordna opptak*).

Other countries have created an institutional framework specifically for planning the transition and linking educational levels and sectors. Denmark has regional guidance centres (*ungdommens uddannelsesvejledning*) that work in conjunction with the institutions to help young adults (19-25 year-olds) as they move to tertiary education and employment, as well as regional guidance centres *(Studievalg)* specifically devoted to the transition to tertiary education. These centres encourage students to identify their centres of interest and to relate them to their aptitudes and skills and the existing offer of training or jobs. They also provide individual coaching for students who have trouble choosing a course of study adapted to their abilities and to the existing offer of training and employment. In France, the *enseignants référents* (teachers in charge of the IEP) co-ordinate and smooth the path between the different types of institutions that upper secondary students attend over the course of their academic career, including tertiary education and access to employment.

The United States would seem to be the only country among those participating in the project to have progressively aimed at developing an integrated transition system for young adults with disabilities. This transition system is based on performance indicators and statistics (such as those supplied by NLTS2) that encourage state and local authorities to include this dimension in their policies and to have at their disposal the data needed to evaluate policies and practices, information useful for local co-operation on a more or less formal basis, and the indicators needed for planning and guiding policies. Indicator No. 13 asks the states to ensure schools' capacity to prepare upper secondary students for tertiary education, and indicator No. 14 gives the situation of students one year after leaving secondary school in terms of their access to tertiary education or employment. This transition system also supports state and institution policies by providing their agencies or authorities with the information and tools needed to optimise their transition practices and/or with the methodologies necessary for planning and implementing the transition process.

The United States has also focused some of its technical assistance for transition on co-ordinating bodies involving the states so as to create network opportunities and national communities of practices in support of initiatives to encourage high school students with disabilities to go on to tertiary education. Networking among state and local players involved in the transition to tertiary education and employment makes it possible to share practical information about initiatives to empower young adults with disabilities and their families, such as peer learning or training for families and teachers. This transition system involves many stakeholders: in addition to teachers, parents and students, there are transition co-ordinators hired at the state level, academic advisors working in the schools, disability support services in universities, vocational rehabilitation counsellors, and employment specialists.

The move towards integrated transition systems

The transition to tertiary education remains difficult

Access to tertiary education still appears to be more difficult and uncertain for young adults with disabilities than for the general population. Growth in the number of students with disabilities is below that of the student population as a whole. While access to tertiary education rose by 8% in Ireland between 2000 and 2006, it increased by only 2.6% for students with disabilities. In the United States, only 45% of young adults with disabilities are in tertiary education four years after leaving secondary school, while the proportion for the general population is 53% (Newman *et al.*, 2009). The French country report indicates that the proportion of secondary school graduates with disabilities who enter tertiary education is only one-quarter that of the general population. In Ireland, young adults with disabilities between the ages of 15 and 29 are only half as likely as the general population of the same age to have a tertiary education diploma (8.3% versus 16%), and of the 1 713 young adults who applied in 2008 for the special arrangements provided by law, only 11.4% were deemed eligible (Higher Education Authority, 2009). In Germany, while enrolments in tertiary education rose by 5% between 2000 and 2006 for the general population, it increased by only 4% for young adults with disabilities (Bundesministerium für Bildung und Forschung, 2007).

As Table 2.2 shows, access to tertiary education seems to be particularly difficult for young adults with a sensory, motor or intellectual impairment; the rise in the number of students with disabilities in tertiary education is due essentially to the rise in the number of students with learning difficulties. In Ireland, the proportion of students with specific learning difficulties recognised by the Fund for Students with Disabilities increased by nearly 2% between 2005 and 2007, to 67.1% of students classed as having a disability; in the United States the proportion of first-year students with a specific learning difficulty rose from 16% of students with disabilities in 1996 to 40% in 2004 (Florian and Rafal, 2008). In Denmark, the proportion with a specific learning difficulty among students receiving disability support rose by 5 percentage points between 2004 and 2006 to 66% of all students with disabilities. In Germany, the proportion of students with allergy problems increased from 52% of the group with health problems in 2000 to 60% in 2006, and the proportion of students with psychological disorders rose by 5% to 11% of the student body (Bundesministerium für Bildung und Forschung, 2007).

Table 2.2. Evolution of the number of students with disabilities, by type of disability

	Denmark		France		Ireland	
	2004	2006	2005	2008	2005	2007
Specific learning difficulty[1]	61.2	66.0	5.4	11.5	64.5	67.1
Mobility impairment	20.2	17.2	20.1	20.5	10.1	7.7
Hearing impairment	6.9	5.4	9.9	8.7	7.0	5.2
Sight impairment	6.4	5.4	14.1	12.4	4.3	3.5
Health-related problems			23.0	19.0	4.7	5.2
Psychological disorders	3.5	4.3	11.2	9.9	1.4	3.1
Multiple disabilities					4.8	4.0
Temporary illness			4.2	4.4		
Other	1.7	1.5	12.1	12.6	3.2	4.2
Total	100.0	100.0	100.0	100.0	100.0	100.0

Note: Denmark: students receiving special education support; France: students who declared a disability; Ireland: students who disclosed a disability.

1. This category corresponds to OECD category CNC B. See Box 1.1.

Source: Denmark: Danish Ministry of Education and Rambøll Management, (2009), "Pathways for Disabled Students to Tertiary Education and Employment", Country background report, Copenhagen; France: Délégation ministérielle à l'emploi des personnes handicapées (2009), "Parcours des personnes handicapées vers l'enseignement supérieur et vers l'emploi", Country background report, ministère de l'Éducation nationale, Paris; Ireland: Higher Education Authority (2009), "OECD Project on Pathways for Disabled Students to Tertiary Education and to Employment", Country background report, Department of Education and Skills, Dublin.

By contrast, in Germany, the proportion of persons declaring a mobility impairment declined by 3% between 2000 and 2006 to 13% of the population of students with disabilities, and the proportion of those with a sensory defect dropped by 4% to 20% (Bundesministerium für Bildung und Forschung, 2007). According to country background reports, a similar decline occurred in Denmark, where the proportion of persons receiving support for an impairment fell by 5% between 2004 and 2006, and in France, where the proportion of students indicating a specific impairment dropped by 6% between 2000 and 2006.

In the United States, the transition to tertiary education varies widely by type of disability. According to NLST2, those with a visual (78%) or hearing (72%) impairment are more likely to attend tertiary education than those with speech/language or other health problems (55%), mobility impairment (54%), learning disabilities (47%), multiple disabilities (35%), emotional disturbances (34%) or mental retardation (27%) (Newman *et al.*, 2009).

These difficulties show that, despite the efforts made, countries find it difficult to create an integrated transition system that:

- makes the move between education levels and sectors part of the mission of secondary schools and universities;

- ensures co-ordination among the levels and sectors of intervention;

- provides financial and methodological incentives as regards transition and empowers young adults with disabilities, institutions and stakeholders involved in the transition process;

- equips stakeholders and systems to take innovative action and pay due attention to the students' future prospects;

- enables young adults with disabilities to meet the demands of tertiary education and employment;

- provides mechanisms and tools for planning, co-ordinating and piloting transition policies and processes.

- is organised within an institutional framework devoted to the transition issue.

Reinforce synergies among actors involved in the transition process

Transition to tertiary education is hindered by a lack of synergies among actors involved in the transition process, owing to the compartmentalisation of the different education levels and of the education and other systems involved in the transition of young adults with disabilities to tertiary education. The lack of linkages between secondary and postsecondary institutions is a major obstacle to the continuity and coherence of their academic career. High schools rarely give universities information about their students, and linkages between institutions often depend on individual initiatives; these may be too sporadic to ensure the co-ordination of institutional strategies needed to build lasting bridges. In Ireland, only two technology institutes in five, for example, have systems for contacting students with disabilities in upper secondary school, and only one in five holds "open house" days targeted specifically at secondary school students with disabilities (Mulvihill, 2005).

This lack of synergies is also related to the absence of co-operation between universities' internal advisory and support services and external support structures, and with families (Newman, 2005; Commission for Social Care Inspection, 2007; Ebersold, 2005; Dee, 2006). This lack of co-operation reinforces the sharp break between administrations dealing with children and adolescents with disabilities and those responsible for supporting and assisting adults. It reinforces the compartmentalisation of those responsible for accessibility at secondary and tertiary education levels and those who define the aid and support related to the compensation of an impairment or to non-academic activities. As a result, stakeholders in the transition process lack an overall vision of the modalities of transition; young adults with disabilities and their families, as noted by Denmark, are obliged to contact many agencies and structures in order to establish the conditions necessary for their studies.

This compartmentalisation may also be linked to a lack of co-ordination at the local level, which makes it difficult to overcome the obstacles raised by the division of responsibilities between sectors and ministries. In Denmark, for example, it impedes co-operation between the Ministry of Education and the Ministry of Tertiary Education and Science, although in fact the responsibility for support and special arrangements in tertiary education falls to the former ministry rather than the latter. Compartmentalisation can also be attributed, as noted by Ireland, to a lack of co-operation between health and/or social affairs ministries and ministries of education or tertiary education. This compartmentalisation may also result, as noted by Norway, from poor territorial integration of co-ordination units or services. It can also be generated, as in the United

States, by a lack of financing, so that vocational rehabilitation agencies lack the resources to provide the aid and support students need to pursue their studies or to find employment upon leaving secondary school.

Optimise training opportunities for actors in the education system

Transition to tertiary education is hampered by a lack of awareness raising and training of the actors involved in the transition process. The initial training of secondary school teachers pays little attention to inclusiveness and pedagogical differentiation. While teachers are for the most part eager to adapt to a diversity of education profiles, they do not always feel well equipped to respond to the pedagogical challenges raised by students with disabilities (OECD, 2009b). The training of Czech teachers is extremely limited in this regard. In Ireland, training for first- and second-level teachers lacks a module on inclusive education. Inclusiveness training is provided essentially through continuing training and is targeted mainly at teachers interested in the issue, as part of the Special Education Support Service (SESS) created by the Department of Education and Skills or as part of the master's programme in special education needs, or through graduate courses offered by certain universities. The continuing training programme for teachers established for 2009-12 places relatively little emphasis on issues or subjects relating to the education of students and young adults with disabilities or specific learning difficulties. While France offers relatively thorough training on inclusive education issues as part of continuing teacher training, initial training of lower and upper secondary teachers devotes very few hours to the education of students with disabilities, so that many teachers feel insufficiently prepared in this area.

Initial and continuing training for personnel involved in the transition of young adults with disabilities from secondary to tertiary education and to employment contains little specific instruction relating to transition mechanisms. The United States is the only participating country to have mentioned training programmes dealing with transitions and targeted at teachers, specialised educators, rehabilitation staff, and guidance counsellors. Their aim is to reinforce their knowledge about transition services, job coaching, vocational education and training courses, competence assessments, partnership co-operation, or working with a special education curriculum that includes transition. By contrast, the inclusive education specialty that France offers secondary school teachers barely touches on transitions, and when it does so it deals primarily with transition to ISCED 3C or 4 courses. The training offered by the Ministries of Health and of Social Affairs to staff in the social and health sectors makes little or no mention of the issues involved in educating students with disabilities or in the pursuit of the training in tertiary education.

This lack of training in inclusive education exposes young adults with disabilities to prejudices on the part of teachers and may deny them the academic skills needed for tertiary education. For example, as noted by Norway and Ireland, teachers may be reluctant to change their teaching practices, especially when they have trouble identifying students with specific learning difficulties as persons who need special pedagogical arrangements and support. Their expectations for students with disabilities may be lower than for other students so that the diploma they obtain may not reflect their actual level of knowledge. In the Czech Republic, several persons interviewed saw this as a major source of these students' failure when they take university entrance examinations and felt that the support and special arrangements for sitting the examinations did not allow for overcoming the academic gap.

As a result of the lack of training in inclusive education, transition to tertiary education may be undermined by the prejudices of professionals involved in defining and implementing the transition process. Some tertiary education students interviewed said, for example, that they had been strongly encouraged to enrol in the humanities and social sciences in order to capitalise on the experience of living with their particular disability rather than to pursue their centres of interest. Others complained that their advisors had lower expectations of them than of other students and had encouraged them to look for a job immediately or to select a professionally less promising course of study.

Increase the incentives offered by funding modes

Transition to tertiary education is also hindered by modes of funding that offer insufficient incentives. By tying eligibility for support and special arrangements to full-time registration, they tend to exclude young adults with more severe and disabling impairments. Moreover, they do not always make it possible to cover accurately the extra costs occasioned by disability, long-term illness, or a specific learning difficulty. They may for example take insufficient account of the additional time students may need or of a change in direction that may become necessary during their studies as a result of disability or illness (SER, 2007). The site visits also showed that access to allowances, bursaries or loans may be more difficult for students with disabilities and that the financial support covered only a portion of the extra costs associated with a disability or illness. In the United States, students with disabilities who are financially dependent on their parents are less likely than other students with disabilities to receive financial aid in the form of grants or loans (Horn and Berktold, 1999). In Germany, resources of students with disabilities in 2006 were close to those of students without disabilities, despite the extra costs implied by their disability or illness (Bundesministerium für Bildung und Forschung, 2007).

The funding that schools receive depends essentially on the academic success of their students to the detriment of their future prospects and the means of facilitating their progress to tertiary education or employment. Schools may thus be inclined to focus on earning a diploma and may not give career guidance counsellors the opportunity to work closely with students or to undertake the necessary multidisciplinary process.

Financial incentives do not always suffice to mobilise tertiary education institutions. Their funding allocations only marginally encourage admissions and support services for students with disabilities to become involved with their environment and to create bridges to actors in secondary schools, the employment sector, the social sector and, if necessary, the health sector in order to combine optimally the different sources of financing needed for the student's success. They may even, given the budgetary pressures generated by the recent economic crisis, be counterproductive. They tend to penalise the institutions that are most receptive to enrolling and supporting students with disabilities and that are particularly attractive to such students, since the funding such institutions receive may not cover the additional costs of enrolling students with disabilities. Opening up to diversity may then appear to be a costly strategy which weighs heavily on the institution's budget.

Their funding may also may not be sufficient to encourage them to invest the amounts needed to make their premises accessible and to ensure the full mobility of students with disabilities on campus. Moreover, the support to institutions does not always reflect the increase in the number of students, especially in tight financial times, and openness to disability may be viewed by institutions as creating a financial risk. In the Czech Republic, for example, the amount allocated to Mazaryk University in Brno for the admission and support of students with disabilities dropped between 2000 and 2008, while the number of students with disabilities it received increased by a factor of six. In Ireland, resources earmarked for the admission and support of students with disabilities have stagnated, while the number of students has been rising on average by 20% a year. Moreover, centralised funding may mean that tertiary education institutions must pay in advance for the required pedagogical adaptations, thereby running a financial risk that some, particularly the smaller ones, can hardly afford. In France, for example the capping of financial assistance provides little incentive for institutions to address the situation of students with complex disabilities, particularly since the delays in the decision-making process of the Departmental Offices for Persons with Disabilities (MDPH) do not allow for identifying clearly the support to which the students are entitled.

Funding modes do not encourage structuring the education process to fit students' educational itinerary and to build the chain of accessibility needed to ensure its continuity and coherence. They offer only limited possibilities for co-ordinating support to compensate for disability or for extracurricular activities that do not fall under the Ministry of Education to the support for access to the institutions under its responsibility. They do not always facilitate access to courses of study that include internships or ensuring workplace adaptations for the internship, especially for short-term internships. This is the case in Norway where employment services and social services do not participate in workplace adaptations for internships. In France the agencies which manage the funds for employment of persons with disabilities in the private sector (*Association de gestion du fonds pour l'insertion professionnelle des personnes handicapées* – AGEFIPH) or the fund for employment of persons with disabilities in the civil service (*Fonds pour l'insertion des personnes handicapées dans la fonction publique* – FIPHFP) are not always ready to support access to internships for young adults with disabilities.

Develop distance learning

Transition to tertiary education is also hindered by the inadequate development of distance learning. This is a very valuable source of accessibility for students with disabilities; they can pursue their studies from home, from a hospital bed, or from a place of rehabilitation. It offers previously rare or non-existent opportunities. It is also a pedagogical resource that is essential to the continuity and success of the academic career, especially in the case of evolving pathologies (mental health problems, for example) that may temporarily interrupt the education process or its extension. Distance learning also constitutes a factor of social inclusion in that it allows students with disabilities to follow their studies from the region in which they live, where they can benefit from the support of family and friends who can help them to overcome the various obstacles they may face in daily life. Lastly, distance education reinforces access to education for those who are in employment or lacking in funds. In Ireland for example, the aim of distance learning is to allow those who are employed or unable to attend a tertiary education institution in the traditional way to have meaningful opportunities to participate.

Yet distance learning seems to have little place in tertiary education institutions' strategies. Few countries mentioned distance learning as a part of their transition policies, and in Norway the number of students engaged in distance learning declined by nearly 40% between 2003 and 2007. In France, the National Centre for Distance Education (CNED) is a public institution that offers academic and professional education to students who cannot attend a regular institution, including those with disabilities. Enrolment is possible at any time of the year; study courses are adapted to the student's needs and the student may obtain pedagogical support from a teacher paid by the agency.

Develop reliable and comparable statistics

Transition to tertiary education is also hindered by policies that take very little account of the future prospects of young adults with disabilities. Countries rarely collect the same data for young adults with disabilities that they collect for young adults without disabilities, making it difficult to determine the impact of anti-discrimination legislation or the effectiveness of the education system's efforts for this group. Few countries have data on the rate of access of young adults with disabilities to secondary or tertiary education, their success rates, their employment upon graduation from secondary or tertiary education, or the social marginalisation of those who are neither in education nor in employment. Where they exist, such data are not always useful for comparison purposes. In the United States, for example, the 26th annual report to Congress indicated that the criteria used to calculate the success rate for secondary school students with disabilities and its trend over time are not the same as those used for students without disabilities (US Department of Education, 2004).

Moreover, few countries know how effective their technical and human support is. Most of the available data shed little light on the academic achievements and future prospects of students enrolled in secondary or tertiary education or on the enabling effect of the additional pedagogical, financial, technical and human resources allocated to them. While it is possible, for example, to identify the additional resources available to high school students with disabilities in Denmark, it is not possible to assess their effectiveness; deaf students or those with hearing problems may therefore be disadvantaged in the education process if the sign language interpreter is poor and cannot be changed during the course of the school year. While French data indicate the number of students with disabilities supported by teacher's assistants, it is not possible to evaluate what they add, so that stakeholders lack the information that would allow them to identify students' progress and the degree of complementarity between the assistants and the teacher.

This lack of data makes it difficult to correlate the allocation of additional resources with the demands of the individual education plan and the support needs identified. In Norway, inadequacies in the definition and implementation of the IEP lead to almost automatic prolongation of secondary schooling for certain types of students with disabilities, even if their educational needs do not justify it. In France and in Ireland, the assignment of a special needs assistant is not always sufficiently correlated with a properly identified educational need, and it is often difficult to assess the assistant's work. In Ireland, the absence of an IEP makes it impossible to relate schooling to precise goals or to determine the impact of the support and special arrangements stipulated by law in terms of learning outcomes or effectiveness. In the Czech Republic, the type of schooling is not explicitly linked to a precise evaluation of students' support needs and this makes the education of students with disabilities more difficult.

Today most countries are unable to identify the quality of the educational paths of young adults with disabilities and the conditions of their access to tertiary education and employment. With the exception of the United States, no country has conducted longitudinal studies to determine the impact of policies on individual academic careers. Identifying individual itineraries and contributing factors is also compromised by differences in the definition of disability between children and adults as well as by the different methods of collecting data. Most often the data collected relate to students who have specifically advised their university of a disability or an educational need rather than to the entire population of university students with special education needs. The understanding of individual itineraries is also compromised by mismatched or overlapping population samples, since the administrative concept of disability used by countries may lead to definitions that vary depending on the administrative authority or educational sector concerned. Indeed, in many cases each authority or body responsible for delivering resources or support to persons with disabilities or institutions defines disability and groups of persons with disabilities in light of the eligibility criteria on which the provision of support depends. In France, data on children and young adults with disabilities correspond to decisions made by the relevant bodies, whereas data on students with disabilities enrolled in tertiary education reflect the number of individuals disclosing their disability or difficulty. This eliminates all those who may need assistance but have not identified themselves, either through ignorance or refusal to be labelled in a particular way.

This lack of data is a serious obstacle to defining and implementing efficient transition policies that require optimisation of resources. The lack of accurate knowledge about the number and the profile of young adults with disabilities creates uncertainty regarding the use of the funding allocated to their education. The lack of data on the impact of policies and the career paths of young adults with disabilities precludes any appreciation of the value added by inclusion policies and the quality of teaching and support practices, and consequently the optimisation of the conditions of admission and support for students with disabilities. Barriers hindering the transition to tertiary education and employment only become very indirectly apparent, via the increase in the number of young adults with disabilities who receive income allowances, or the rise in the number of unemployed persons with disabilities who no longer look for jobs (OECD, 2006). Barriers may also bring to light information that is primarily qualitative, unsystematic or even anecdotal, as when teachers and support staff see the failure of students with disabilities as a result of a lack of the necessary adaptations or support.

According to the Center on Education Policy, the need for reliable data is particularly important in the United States where high school students will be required, as of 2012, to validate their secondary education by passing an "exit exam" that will be common to all students. Despite accommodations and/or alternate assessment opportunities, the examination may be more demanding than current ones and could lead to academic failure for disadvantaged students (Center on Education Policy, 2007).

Develop new piloting tools and improve those that exist

Transition to tertiary education is also hampered by the lack of tools for piloting the transition process or the inadequacy of those that exist. The centralisation of university enrolment applications is not sufficient to co-ordinate and pilot the transition process, which is not always based on an IEP. With the exception of Denmark and the United States, no country requires secondary schools to include the transition issue in their individual education plans, and institutions are thus deprived of a valuable piloting tool.

Including a transition plan in the IEP encourages institutions to make transition a component of their institutional policy and to integrate it pragmatically into their approach to the curriculum, their evaluation methods, and their guidance counselling. It also encourages institutions to be open to their environment and to take initiatives to obtain the information needed to provide support and coaching for students with disabilities, to make those responsible for transition aware of the specific characteristics of students with disabilities, to encourage university personnel to become involved in support work, and perhaps to include in their course of study a component directly related to transition. They can develop strategies combining the educational approach to disability promoted by the social model of disability with the diagnostic approach and involving, if necessary, the disability service providers that may contribute to the student's transition plan. As noted in Norway, such strategies help to avoid overly automatic extensions of course duration for students with disabilities.

The existence of a transition plan encourages students with disabilities to think about their future at an early stage and to consider what is needed to achieve their goal. It also serves to formalise the different stages in the transition process and to mobilise appropriately the actors who contribute at different moments to the continuity and coherence of their itinerary. It also makes it possible, if necessary, to enlist parents' interest in the future of their child and to encourage them to participate in meetings, to consider the role they may play, and to acquire the skills they may need. In addition, a transition plan allows for mobilising the tools and methodologies for supporting young adults with disabilities in their career and for equipping them with a document specifying their skills and giving information about their impairment and the arrangements and support required in tertiary education.

Piloting the transition process is also hindered by the absence of an institutional framework specifically devoted to the transition issue or, as observed for Denmark's municipal and regional guidance services, by an institutional framework that takes sufficient account of the particularities of young adults with disabilities. The agencies responsible for co-ordinating the education process do not always address the question of transition. For instance, in Ireland, the special education needs organisers generally have little contact with tertiary education institutions, and in France the student advisors (*enseignants référents*) have too many students with disabilities to look after to be able to fully cover transition issues as a part of their work. The methodological tools and guides prepared for institutions and students with disabilities and their families do not always suffice to ensure that all those involved in the transition process are working towards the same objectives and co-ordinating their actions. Multidisciplinary co-ordination structures are not always able to organise the transition process around precise and measurable objectives in terms of outcomes and the piloting tools to ensure them.

Services specifically dedicated to the transition issue can also supplement the information provided by methodological guides and tools and support institutions as well as students with disabilities throughout the process. Where they exist, these services make it easier to work with the persons most in need of guidance. Teachers responsible for transition do not always have the time to ensure the flow of information among those involved in the transition plan. These services may also act as resource centres to help students with disabilities to disclose their disability or their specific learning difficulty, to ensure the continuity of support, and to work towards the commitment and involvement of all those concerned by the transition process.

Conclusion

The opportunities for access to tertiary education for young adults with disabilities have improved noticeably in recent years as a result of the inclusion policies which have allowed a growing number of pupils with disabilities or a specific learning difficulty to obtain the level of education required to enter tertiary education. Inclusion policies forbid discrimination based on disability and promote an educational approach to disability which focuses on the ability of education systems to meet the needs of young adults with disabilities. They have encouraged secondary and tertiary education institutions to include disability issues in their policies. They have also mobilised technical, human and financial resources so that institutions can ensure accessibility and young adults with disabilities can have the same access and opportunities to succeed as their non-disabled peers.

The increasing numbers of students with disabilities enrolled in tertiary education also results from policies requiring education systems to focus on each student's success, to create flexible educational environments adapted to the diversity of educational needs, to fight dropout and to include quality assurance issues in their policies. It reflects, in addition, the growing mobilisation of education systems around students' prospects as a result of the creation of services focused on transition issues and of the multiplication of bridges between educational levels and sectors.

However, policies face difficulties for dealing with the careers of young adults with disabilities beyond secondary education, as their opportunities for access to tertiary education are more uncertain, especially for those with sensory, motor or cognitive impairments. These difficulties suggest that, despite progress made, education policies could be improved by developing integrated transition systems to encourage schools to be aware of each pupil's prospects, by empowering stakeholders and systems, by facilitating the development of bridges between educational levels and sectors and of local synergies so as to mobilise young adults with disabilities around their future.

References

Bjerkan, K.Y. and M. Veenstra (2008), Utdanning, arbeid, bolig og transport for unge voksne 20 til 35 år. In *Statusrapport 08: samfunnsutviklingen for personer med nedsatt funksjonsevne*, Nasjonalt dokumentasjonssenter for personer med nedsatt funksjonsevne, Oslo, pp. 154-207.

Bundesministerium für Bildung und Forschung (2007), *Die wirtschaftliche und soziale Lage der Studierenden in der Bundesrepublik Deutschland 2006*; 18. Sozialerhebung des Deutschen Studentenwerks durchgeführt durch HIS Hochschul-Informations-System, Bonn/Berlin.

Center on Education Policy (2007), *State High School Exit Exams: Working to Raise Test Scores*, Center on Education Policy, Washington, DC.

Commission for Social Care Inspection (2007), *Growing up Matters: Better Transition Planning for Young People with Complex Needs*, Danske Studerendes Faellesrad (2008), vi er jo ikke en delaf universitetes bevidsthed, Copenhagen.

Danish Ministry of Education and Rambøll Management (2009), "Pathways for Disabled Students to Tertiary Education and Employment", Country background report, Denmark, Copenhagen

Dee, L. (2006), *Improving Transition Planning for Young People with Special Educational Needs,* Open University Press, Maidenhead.

Délégation ministérielle à l'emploi des personnes handicapées (2009), "Parcours des personnes handicapées vers l'enseignement supérieur et vers l'emploi", Country background report, ministère de l'Éducation nationale, Paris.

Department of Public Instruction, Department of Workforce Development, Department of Health Services (2009), *Seamless Collaboration with and for Students with Disabilities; Transitioning to Employment and Adult Life*, Wisconsin Department of Public Instruction.

Douglas, J.A. (2004), "Dynamique de la massification et de la différenciation : comparaison des systèmes d'enseignement supérieur du Royaume-Uni et de la Californie", *Politiques et gestion de l'enseignement supérieur,* Vol. 16, No. 3, OECD, Paris.

Dyson, A. (2008), "Transitions for Disabled and Vulnerable Young People in the United Kingdom", Background paper for the OECD, University of Manchester.

Ebersold, S. (2005), *Le temps des servitudes. La famille à l'épreuve du handicap*, PUR, Rennes.

Florian, L. and J. Rafal (2008), "Transitions of People with Disabilities Beyond Secondary Education in the United States", Background paper for the OECD, University of Aberdeen and Cambridge University.

Galland, O. and P. Rouault (1996), "Des études supérieures inégalement rentables selon les milieux sociaux", *INSEE première* No. 469, July.

Higher Education Authority (2009), *Higher Education Key Facts and Figures 07/08*, Dublin.

Horn, L. and J. Berktold (1999), *Students with Disabilities in Postsecondary Education: A Profile of Preparation, Participation, and Outcomes*, US Department of Education, National Center for Education Statistics, Washington, DC.

Horn, L. and S. Nevill (2006), *Profile of Undergraduates in U.S. Postsecondary Education Institutions: 2003–04: With a Special Analysis of Community College Students* (NCES 2006-184), US Department of Education, National Center for Education Statistics, Washington, DC.

Legard, S. (2009), "Pathways from Education to Work for Young People with Impairments and Learning Difficulties in Norway", Work Research Institute, Oslo.

Ministère de l'Éducation nationale, ministère de l'Enseignement supérieur et de la Recherche (2010), *Repères et références statistiques sur les enseignements, la formation et la recherche*, La documentation française, Paris.

Ministère de l'Enseignement supérieur et de la Recherche (2010), *Effectifs des étudiants handicapés en universités*, Paris.

Ministry of Education of the Czech Republic (2009), "Transitions to Tertiary Education and to Employment for Young People with Impairments and Learning Difficulties", Country background report, Ministry of Education of the Czech Republic, Prague.

Mulvihill, R. (2005), *Participation of and Services for Students with Disabilities in Institutes of Technology*, AHEAD.

National Center for Education Statistics (NCES) (2009), *Digest of Education Statistics 2008*, US Department of Education, Washington, DC.

National Center on Secondary Education and Transition (2000), *Students with Disabilities in Postsecondary Education: A Profile of Preparation, Participation, and Outcomes*. Institute for Educational Sciences, Washington, DC.

National Center on Secondary Education and Transition (2004), *Current Challenges Facing the Future of Secondary Education and Transition Services for Youth with Disabilities in the United States*, US Department of Education, Office of Special Education Program, Washington, DC.

Newman, L. (2005), *Family Involvement in the Educational Development of Youth with Disabilities. A Special Topic Report of Findings from the National Longitudinal Transition Study 2 (NLTS2)*, SRI International, Menlo Park, CA.

Newman, L. *et al.* (2009), *The Post-High School Outcomes of Youth with Disabilities up to 4 Years After High School*, SRI International, Menlo Park, CA.

OECD (1999), *Inclusive Education at Work: Students with Disabilities in Mainstream Schools*, OECD, Paris.

OECD (2003), *Disability in Higher Education*, OECD, Paris.

OECD (2004), *Internationalisation and Trade in Higher Education: Opportunities and Challenges*, OECD, Paris.

OECD (2005), *Students with Disabilities, Learning Difficulties and Disadvantages: Statistics and Indicators*, OECD, Paris.

OECD (2006), *Sickness, Disability and Work: Breaking the Barriers, Volume 1: Norway, Poland and Switzerland*, OECD, Paris.

OECD (2007), *Students with Disabilities, Learning Difficulties and Disadvantages: Policies, Statistics and Indicators*, OECD, Paris.

OECD (2009a), *Education at a Glance: OECD Indicators*, OECD, Paris.

OECD (2009b), *Creating Effective Teaching and Learning Environments: First Results from TALIS*, OECD, Paris.

PricewaterhouseCoopers (2007),"Review of Further Education Provision for Learners (16-25 year-olds) with Learning Difficulties and/or Disabilities in the North West", *http://readingroom.lsc.gov.uk/lsc/NorthWest/LLDD_Report_Finalweb_1.pdf*, accessed 9 February 2008.

Selz, M. and L.A. Vallet (2006), "La démocratisation de l'enseignement et son paradoxe apparent", in Insee, *Données sociales,* La documentation française, Paris.

SER (2007), *Meedoen zonder beperkingen. Meer participatiemogelijkheden voor jonggehandicapten. Sociaal Economische Raad*, Advies rapport No. 6, SER, The Hague.

Statistics Norway (2007), *Ungdoms levekår, Tor Morten Normann (red.)*, Statistisk sentralbyrå, Oslo.

UNESCO (1994), *The Salamanca Statement and Framework for Action*, UNESCO, Paris.

United Nations Organization (UNO) (2006), *UN Convention on Rights of Persons with Disabilities,* UNO, New York.

US Department of Education (2004), *Twenty-sixth Annual Report to Congress on the Implementation of the Individuals with Disabilities Education Act*, U.S. Census Bureau, Survey of Income and Program Participation, June–September 2005, *www.ed.gov/about/reports/annual/osep/2004/index.html*, accessed 11 February 2007.

US Department of Education (2010), *Department of Education Fiscal Year 2010 Congressional Action*, *www.ed.gov/about/overview/budget/budget10/10action.pdf*.

Wagner, M. *et al.* (2005), *After High School: A First Look at the Postschool Experiences of Youth with Disabilities,* A report from the National Longitudinal Transition Study-2 (NLTS2), SRI International, Menlo Park, CA.

World Health Organization (WHO) (2001), *International Classification of Functioning, Disability and Health,* World Health Organization, Geneva.

Chapter 3

Institutional strategies to support students with disabilities

The transition to tertiary education depends on secondary schools' strategies to prepare young adults with disabilities to cope with the demands of tertiary education and on the admissions strategies of tertiary education institutions to facilitate their success. It is important in this respect for schools to support young adults with disabilities throughout the transition process by allowing them to choose their courses with full knowledge of the facts, by encouraging them to plan the various stages in the transition process and by preparing them to play an active role in their future. Furthermore, it is important for admissions strategies of tertiary education institutions to take steps to avoid the risk of failure and to incorporate support procedures into a contract focused on imparting skills to students with disabilities. The transition to tertiary education is predicated on rooting the admission and follow-up of students with disabilities in an inclusive ethos able to mobilise the entire university community around the diversity of educational profiles and the success of every student.

Introduction

The transition to tertiary education depends greatly on the strategies adopted by educational institutions to prepare secondary school students for the demands of tertiary education. It also depends on the admissions and support strategies implemented by tertiary education institutions to ensure that students are well integrated and can succeed.

This chapter first describes the factors affecting the paths to tertiary education as they appear from an analysis of the work of upper secondary schools to prepare high school students for tertiary education and the admissions strategies developed by institutions. It then describes the factors that facilitate or impede the progress and success of students with disabilities in tertiary education in light of an analysis of support strategies in tertiary education institutions. It builds upon information provided during interviews during the site visits and by countries' background reports.

The bumpy road to tertiary education

Help students to plan their route

The work of secondary education schools to prepare upper secondary students for tertiary education depends on the importance attached to the question of transition in education policies. It is more important in countries such as the United States or Denmark, which have made transition a component of the education system. It is much less important in countries such as the Czech Republic or Norway, which include it very indirectly in the institutional mission, or such as France, which have included it only very recently. In Ireland, for example, preparing for the requirements of tertiary education, particularly in terms of accessibility, can be hampered by the fact that funding for support is conditioned upon the enrolment of the young adults with disabilities in tertiary education.

The quality of the work performed to prepare upper secondary students for tertiary education differs among institutions. The coherence and continuity of the student's path will depend on the policies adopted, the quality of management, and the degree of commitment on the part of the institution. While some students in the United States interviewed during the site visit believed they had been well prepared in high school for the demands of tertiary education, others felt that their high school had not prepared them, or had done so inadequately, and both groups stressed the importance of the commitment of individual school staff. Danish students interviewed indicated that the path to tertiary education varied; some secondary schools included the question of disability or a specific learning difficulty in their policy while others did not, or to a lesser extent. French students pointed to the differences among education advisors (*enseignants référents*) in terms of preparation and support for tertiary education.

Despite these disparities, institutional strategies seem to include some important common elements for preparing upper secondary school students for tertiary education and employment and for helping them to take charge of their future and cope with the upheavals and setbacks ahead. These elements include making students aware of the implications of the move to tertiary education and the steps involved, encouraging them to look at existing training options in light of employment opportunities and their centres of interest and aptitudes, and to plan as early and as methodically as possible for the different stages in the transition process.

Make informed choices about courses or employment opportunities

Upper secondary schools seek to allow students with disabilities to make informed choices and to select the course of study that is best adapted to their situation and professionally the most effective. As for any other student, this involves providing them with objective information about the content and the prerequisites of the studies they wish to pursue, the occupations these may lead to, and the prospects they may offer for employment, so that students can choose a course of study appropriate to their centres of interest and/or an institution appropriate to their particular needs. It also involves encouraging students to think about their centres of interest, the kind of work they wish to do, the objectives they wish to achieve, and the career they wish to pursue. This information can be conveyed through handbooks and documents distributed to students, such as those of the French national office on information on programme courses and careers *(Office national d'information sur les enseignements et les professions –* ONISEP*)*, or during campus visits, information meetings or events at which young adults can meet potential employers or university representatives. According to the country reports, this can also involve, as in Denmark, courses that include labour market as well as vocational education and training issues or, as in the United States, sessions to familiarise pupils with disabilities in grade 9 with the academic demands of tertiary education and to encourage them to prepare for it. Teaching programmes may also include, as in the Czech Republic, specific courses on choosing employment or entering tertiary education.

Information to upper secondary students can also be delivered through meetings in the course of their studies with representatives of tertiary education and the world of employment at which they can discuss their career expectations and prospects. According to some students interviewed, such meetings make them aware of the academic requirements of tertiary education as well as the behavioural skills required to obtain their rights, organise their time or plan their work. Students also attach importance to a "discovery route" which, as in Denmark, encourages them to gain information on existing opportunities and to examine their choices in light of their aptitudes with their advisors and gradually develop a project which makes of the transition process a continuous discovery of education opportunities and their impact in terms of employment.

Information furnished to upper secondary students with disabilities deals more rarely with the degree of accessibility of tertiary education institutions and the means of obtaining support and special accommodations and their effectiveness. This type of information is useful not only for gearing the choice of study to students' centres of interest and aptitudes but also for appreciating the conditions they will face and their opportunities in terms of studies. Norwegian students said that information about an institution's accessibility would allow them to estimate more accurately the financial risk inherent in enrolling in a particular university or course of study. Some American students said they had avoided applying for courses that did not offer sufficient assurance in terms of accessibility because they recognised that this could raise the risk of failure. Information of this kind also ensures timely submission of enrolment applications and requests for special support and arrangements. Networking via the Internet is another source of valuable information which allows upper secondary students to exchange experience and solutions with their peers throughout the transition process, to find answers to their questions from university personnel and even to find common solutions to problems also encountered by others.

Plan the transition to tertiary education and employment

In addition, strategies developed to prepare high school students with disabilities for tertiary education and employment encourage them, to varying extents, to plan the various steps in the transition process and to adapt their objectives and needs as the situation evolves. These steps may be set out explicitly in handbooks and methodological tools prepared for students with disabilities, as in the case of George Washington University (Washington, DC) through its HEATH Resource Center. This handbook is designed to lead students, their families and their counsellors to identify the steps in the transition process, to be aware of potential obstacles, and to understand the support and arrangements that will be needed and the partners that may be involved. These steps may also be explained by teachers or guidance counsellors during group or individual meetings.

As noted in the reports of the Czech Republic, Ireland and Norway, this planning can be done through the more or less formal contacts that students have with universities, on the advice of their teachers or counsellors, who urge them to contact as early as possible the university of their choice in order to prepare this step carefully and calmly. It can be done, as in the United States, through a transition plan worked out jointly by a multidisciplinary team in conjunction with the student's individual education plan (IEP), and regularly revised. As in Denmark, and more recently in France, it can be stretched out over the course of upper secondary education in order to support the students throughout the process. Planning may also be carried out by external co-ordination services which are tasked with ensuring continuity by putting the student in touch with the university, by working to overcome any reluctance the university may express, or by mobilising stakeholders that may help students obtain the financial, medical or paramedical support to which they are entitled.

Prepare students to take charge of their future

Strategies developed by upper secondary schools aim also, albeit to varying degrees, to prepare young adults with disabilities to cope with the demands of tertiary education and employment. Schools make them aware of the changes implied by the passage to adulthood and indicate how to cope with these changes by describing the procedures they will have to follow to receive support. They will urge students, more or less strongly, to disclose their special education needs as soon as possible to the university they have chosen, so that accessibility arrangements can be identified and implemented in a timely manner.

In the United States, disability support services aim at preparing high school students to take responsibility for their future, make their rights known and ensure that their needs are met by developing self-advocacy skills. To this end, they are advised to involve students in defining and implementing an individual education plan, to make them aware of the need to focus as early as possible on their future beyond secondary education, to include this in an individual transition plan, and to advise them about the passage to adulthood. Schools also inform students about the conditions governing their rights and their associated duties. They encourage students to identify their strengths and weaknesses, with the help of a teacher or a counsellor, the areas in which they need to progress further, the support and accommodations they require, and services they may need. By participating in transition planning meetings, young adults with disabilities will be better prepared to indicate their educational needs, defend their rights, deal with conflicts, and take an active interest in their future throughout the transition process.

The approach to empowering students with respect to their future varies. Danish schools pay less attention to fostering self-advocacy and more to making informed and reasonable choices. The country report indicates that pedagogical adaptation includes coaching and advice for families and upper secondary students who need and want it, and the Danish transition support services are required to advise the students regarding their choices and ensure that they are in a position to pursue them upon graduation.

Other countries also encourage students to take charge of their future, although the approach is less central and perhaps more recent. The support services available to French upper secondary students with disabilities are designed to make them as independent as possible and to help them construct an academic career as close as possible to their centres of interest, but it is not their task to teach students to fight for their rights or the quality of their implementation. In Norway, the first task of the education and psychology services (*PP-tjenesten*) and the national support system (*Staped*) is to enhance students' independence by helping them to cope with their disability and its consequences, but self-advocacy is not a primary objective. In the Czech Republic, transition is not the responsibility of the Ministry of Education and the support available to upper secondary students rarely takes account of their future career. Ireland recently developed guidance programmes in schools to provide information on subject and programme choices and the corresponding career implications. These programmes aim at enabling students to make an objective assessment of their interests and aptitudes and relate the to further education and training and career areas. They promote study and self-management skills, career investigation, job search and interview skills, as well as use of available information and communication technology (ICT) tools as learning aids. Schools thereby develop a range of linkages with further and higher education and training institutions and employers, and guidance counsellors are linked with access/disability officers in tertiary education institutions and with the vocational training services provided by FAS (Ireland's National Training and Employment Authority), and the health sector.

Emphasise guidance rather than information

However, strategies developed by secondary schools do not seem to prepare students with disabilities for the demands of tertiary education very effectively. They tend to provide information rather than accompany the students throughout the process. This is particularly true in countries in which schooling is not based on an individual education plan, or when those plans are too imprecise for building a transition based on a student's achievements and the continuity of his or her course of study. Site visits showed that, without an IEP, schools find it difficult to build a transition process that allows young adults to make a knowledgeable choice of course of study and to be aware as early as possible of the demands of the labour market and tertiary education. Nor will the teachers have an overall vision allowing them to take a holistic approach to the education process and to build, as suggested by research, a dynamic involving the family and other stakeholders in the transition process. In Ireland, for example, some students complained that special needs assistants and visiting teachers did not always provide the support or the pedagogical materials needed to prepare them for tertiary education requirements because they did not have an IEP. This is also the case in the Czech Republic, where the lack of information on existing technological support and the lack of training in innovative teaching methods prevent upper secondary schools from being more open to students with disabilities and facilitating their academic success.

The work to prepare upper secondary students for entering tertiary education does not seem to include other stakeholders that may contribute to a holistic approach and to an effective transition. Schools seem insufficiently or too informally integrated into their environment to be able to mobilise the sources of information and advice that can make teachers better aware of transition issues and encourage them to see a student's future as a component of his or her academic success. Transition advisors may also lack the time to combine their teaching work with counselling and support. They may also be inadequately equipped for the tasks demanded of them. The United States and, to a lesser extent, Ireland are the only countries to have prepared methodological guidance for those involved in the transition process, and to have developed networks for exchanging knowledge and experience so that professionals, students and their families are aware of the skills and qualities required in tertiary education.

Interviewed students also mentioned a lack of support at the end of secondary school which left them with a feeling of isolation, particularly if they were away from home and thus deprived of informal support for overcoming housing or transport problems, difficulties due to the lack of accessibility to the pedagogical environment as well as those resulting from a lack of co-operation among the players involved in the transition process. This lack of support was noted particularly in Norway and Denmark, where student services lack the training and tools that would allow them to meet the needs of students with a disability or a specific learning difficulty. In Denmark, for example, transition support services do not always include these students in their strategies. The Copenhagen service visited provided support to 812 young adults with disabilities in 2008 (or 4.8% of the total population served) and, at the time of the visit, it had no documentation adapted for students with a visual impairment or a learning difficulty, and no possibility of sign language translation for deaf students. In Norway, the university career centres are not always sufficiently aware of and trained for dealing with particularities linked with a disability or a specific learning difficulty; they may be unable to advise students with disabilities properly or to work out strategies with employers for integrating them. In the United States, school staff report that about 70% of students with IEPs participate actively by providing input (58%) or taking a leadership role (12%). Yet about 6% of secondary schools students with disabilities reportedly do not attend IEP or transition meetings and nearly 20% of secondary schools students with disabilities have programmes that are only somewhat well suited or not at all well suited to their transition goals (Cameto *et al.*, 2004).

The site visits also showed that the information supplied is, for the most part, very similar to that provided to the student body as a whole, especially when, as in Norway or Denmark, countries do not have specific measures for young adults with disabilities. Students complained, for example, that they were not sufficiently informed about the degree of accessibility of tertiary education institutions in order to include this information in their choices. Some students interviewed in the Czech Republic said they discovered too late that some universities were not accessible, and were therefore obliged to register in universities further away; the need to travel long distances daily increased their level of fatigue and reduced their chances of success. Others regretted that the lack of support during the transition process made it difficult to manage factors that can lead to discontinuities. This was the case, for example, of French students who complained that they had learned too late of their admission to tertiary education to present a timely application for support to the Departmental Offices for Persons with Disabilities (MDPH) and that they had to wait several months to learn whether they could follow the chosen course of study and obtain the necessary support. Many students also indicated that they had been destabilised by the barriers they progressively discovered when applying for support and the special arrangements stipulated by law, despite the existence of guidebooks and other printed materials.

Strategies aiming at preparing upper secondary students for tertiary education and employment also too frequently overlook the negative impact of transport and housing issues. These factors are considered major obstacles by young adults with disabilities, especially those with impaired mobility (Bjerkan and Veenstra, 2008). Access to housing may indeed be affected by a shortage of physically or financially accessible housing as well as by student housing allocation policies that do not include disability issues sufficiently in their criteria. Access to transport can be made more difficult by financial constraints and long waiting times, particularly for specially adapted vehicles. It may also be hindered by time constraints imposed by relatively inaccessible public transport and the lack of suitably adapted transport. For example, the lack of suitable transport and support led nearly 8% of the student cohort tracked by the NLTS2 survey to abandon their studies (Newman *et al.*, 2009).

By giving more importance to information than to providing guidance to students with disabilities during the transition process, upper secondary schools tend to delegate to them the responsibility for the effectiveness and quality of their transition. They may thus undermine initiatives to urge students to take responsibility for their future since many students consider that these skills are not always sufficient to overcome barriers resulting from institutional obstacles over which they have no control. Upper secondary schools also tend to make parents' involvement the key driver of the transition to tertiary education. Families do of course help to overcome the lack of co-ordination between agencies and the lack of co-operation among professionals, to circumvent bureaucratic obstacles, to arrange access to internships or vocational training courses, and to maintain the student's motivation. While parents may help, they can also thwart the desire for independence of young adults with disabilities and stand in the way of the autonomy generally required by tertiary education institutions or the labour market. Moreover, as parents are often merely informed about the decisions taken rather than actively involved in the process, they may not be able to assume the responsibilities imposed on them (Wagner *et al.*, 2005; Ebersold, 2005).

Base tertiary education admissions strategies on a support plan

Transition to tertiary education also hinges on the admissions strategies of tertiary education institutions. These strategies vary widely, depending on the institution and the rationale underlying education policies (Ebersold, 2008). Yet, regardless of the institutional approach, disability support services tend to base their admissions strategy for students with disabilities on common principles, designed essentially to secure students' active commitment to their chosen course of study, to ensure their inclusion into the university community, to take the steps necessary to facilitate their success, and to guarantee the quality of the special arrangements made. These principles aim at preventing the risk of failure, at empowering the students, and at basing the support plan on a contractual relationship between the tertiary education institution and the student.

Prevent the risk of failure

Preventing failure is one component of these admissions strategies. Disability support services may therefore take into consideration the various extracurricular dimensions that also contribute to a student's success. They may seek to involve the family in the study and support plan in order to ensure continuity of support and maintain the student's motivation. They may also ensure close collaboration among the services responsible for transport, housing and financial assistance and include in the support plan the various elements that may influence the student's progress. In France, the linkages that exist, for example, between the School for Advanced Research in the Social Sciences (*École des Hautes Études en Sciences Sociales* – EHESS*)* and the Regional Centre for School and University Support *(Centre régional des œuvres universitaires et scolaires* – CROUS), the Service for Home Education and Care *(Service d'éducation et de soins spécialisés à domicile* – SESSAD) and the Departmental Offices for Persons with Disabilities (MDPH) prevent students with disabilities from being hindered in their study by problems of housing, transport or home services. In order to facilitate continuity and coherence, institutions such as Ireland's Limerick Institute of Technology have entered into agreements with other universities and non-tertiary postsecondary institutions as well as institutions that have students with disabilities who have followed alternative educational routes. In the United States, Montgomery College (Maryland) includes the transition to university in its admissions and support strategy and negotiates agreements with selected universities to this end.

Disability support services also consider it essential to replicate or prolong the preparatory work undertaken in secondary school, especially for students with disabilities who may become more vulnerable during their school career, or for those whose special arrangements have led to differences in their writing skills or their ability to be rigorous or to work as compared with average students. Most tertiary education institutions participate for this purpose in "open doors" days, information sessions organised by high schools or job fairs in order to inform students about programmes and courses offered, admission procedures, disability support services and the need to contact this service as early as possible. Some disability support services collaborate with secondary school staff to obtain additional information on students' academic level, their potential and personality and to make sure they are aware of the courses offered and the strategy to be pursued. Some French universities rely on centralised post-baccalaureate admissions files established by academic inspectorates to identify students at risk and offer support tailored to their profile. Interviews during the site visit in the United States showed that the HEATH Resource Center at George Washington University has prepared a "toolkit" for high school guidance and career counsellors. It offers ideas and strategies to help them anticipate and prevent potential obstacles to transition; it urges them, when counselling students with disabilities, to focus on their personal interests rather than on specific programmes that may be available, and it relates the role of the counsellor in the transition process to that of the student, the parents and other stakeholders.

However, relatively few institutions seek to develop and formalise co-operative relationships with upper secondary schools. Some tertiary education institutions may intervene in the course of study offered by the secondary school or, as in the United States, may propose modules for the secondary school curriculum that can be validated in tertiary education. Others may establish contractual links with secondary schools and upper secondary students based on a transition plan for which the university agrees to monitor the student regularly, propose changes to the course of study if it is found unsuitable, and keep the upper secondary teacher informed annually of the student's progress until he or she finds employment.

Empower new arrivals

Empowering students with disabilities is another component of admissions strategies. This involves encouraging them to disclose their specific circumstances so as to ensure timely access to the support to which they are entitled. It seems essential to treat their support and special arrangements as far as possible as normal and to dissociate disability from any medical definition, given that students with disabilities do not consider themselves "sick". For example, the University of Paris 8 has attached the disability support service to the university president's office and its administrative services, rather than to the preventive medicine or social services. The University of Copenhagen ensures that pedagogical accessibility initiatives take account of all students, whatever their particular circumstances, which may include a disability or learning difficulty. In Dublin, tertiary education institutions ensure data confidentiality and send teachers and staff only a summary of essential information on students with disabilities. Some universities try to help students with disabilities to cope with the requirements imposed on them. George Washington University gives applicants with disabilities tools and handbooks to help them see the advantages of disclosing their special need and defining a strategy to avoid being stigmatised, to participate actively in identifying support and special arrangements, and to see that they are properly implemented. Trinity College Dublin and Montgomery College both try to put students with disabilities in contact with peers who may, if necessary, act as tutors.

This empowerment relies on information and counselling regarding the organisation of the course of study, the institution's accessibility policy, the support and special arrangements available, and the requirements that must be met. The information can be provided in documents posted on the Internet, handbooks or interviews with personnel from the disability support office. In Norway, the University of Oslo's Internet site invites students with disabilities to consult the website of the disability support service to learn about its principles and purposes, its services, eligibility criteria, and application procedures. Aarhus University in Denmark has prepared a handbook for students with disabilities with detailed information on its disability support service, the different categories of students eligible for support, and the procedures governing admission as well as access to support, by type of impairment. The French Ministry of Higher Education and Research has published a handbook on the support and special arrangements available for students with disabilities in French universities. Trinity College Dublin, like many other institutions, holds a meeting for students who have disclosed an educational need and has prepared an information guide as well as various electronic tools. It encourages students to familiarise themselves with academic requirements, to be aware that special aids and arrangements do not by themselves guarantee success, to contact the education advisors to learn about the requirements that must be met, and to avoid becoming a risk to themselves or others. The disability support service of George Washington University provides a document for new students to advise them on time management, the skills expected of students, learning strategies adapted to the university environment, and essential questions to ask.

Information and advice can also take the form of training sessions. Some American tertiary education institutions offer "college survival courses" to make new arrivals aware of the academic demands of tertiary education, the self-advocacy skills they need as well as those required to manage their time and workload. Montgomery College has developed a special programme to integrate students with disabilities into the university community. At any point during the transition process, students with disabilities may turn to the programme and locate remedial courses in certain subjects, arrange for support from tutors, and acquire the skills needed to pursue tertiary education studies. Masaryk University in Brno (Czech Republic) holds two-day information sessions for new students, including those with a disability or a specific learning difficulty, to present the courses of study, faculties and information systems and to introduce them to their fellow students. Information can also be conveyed through specific support; for example, the University of Paris 8 (France) provides one or more sign language interpreters to deaf students during "open door" days. Some French universities offer students who have maintained their initial choice, despite advice to the contrary, the services of a personal monitor who will provide advice throughout the first semester and to whom the student may turn in case of difficulty.

Develop a contractual relationship between the student and the university

Establishing a contractual relationship between the student and the university is another important aspect of the admissions strategies of disability support services. This contractual relationship is intended to secure the commitment of the student and the institution to a support plan specifying the objectives, the resources, the arrangements involved and the conditions of implementation.

This contractual relationship implies identifying the student's eligibility. The student must provide a medical certificate documenting the existence of a disability, a chronic illness or a specific learning difficulty. Some universities rely on this certificate to evaluate educational needs. Trinity College Dublin asks students with a specific learning difficulty to provide a recent psychological report (within the last three years), indicating the student's intellectual age and reading level, in order to determine the academic impact of the impairment, identify the support and arrangements needed, ensure their financing, and discuss their implementation with faculty teaching teams. Other universities rely on this medical certificate to implement the means recommended by the physician. The certificate requested by the Limerick Institute of Technology must detail the student's impairment and indicate its impact in terms of the academic requirements and the necessary special support and arrangements. The University of Paris 8 asks students to visit the preventive medicine service so that the physician can specify the arrangements required (extra testing time, secretarial assistance, composition in a private room, use of specific materials, etc.) (Figure 3.1). Montgomery College requires the certificate to indicate the disability and its severity, the procedures and methods used for the diagnosis, the student's functional limitations in terms of education, and a certificate declaring that the disability or specific learning difficulty substantially limits the activities of daily life (hearing, seeing, speaking, learning) and recommending special arrangements. Still other universities, such as those of Copenhagen, Aarhus or Brno, have educational needs assessed by associations or agencies specialised in the particular disability in question. Aarhus University arranges for testing to determine special education needs, conducted for example by a lexicologist when a student presents a specific learning difficulty or by a physician in case of a mental health problem.

Figure 3.1. Procedure for identifying needs and support for students with disabilities in France

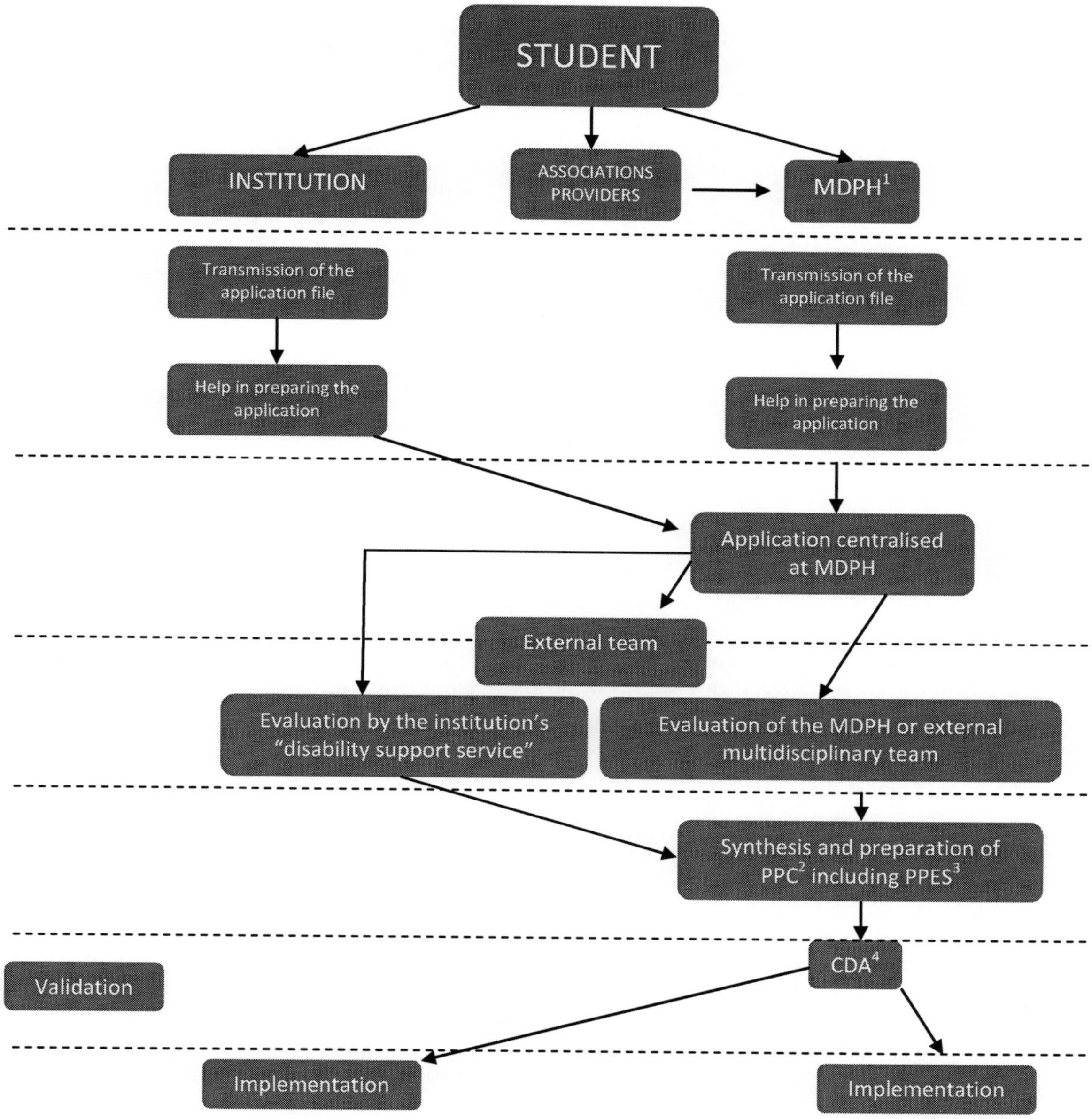

1. Departmental Offices for Persons with Disabilities (*Maisons départementales des personnes handicapées*).

2. Personalised compensation plan.

3. Personalised higher education plan.

4. Commission on Rights and Autonomy.

Source: Conférence des Présidents d'Université (2007), "Guide de l'accueil de l'étudiant handicapé à l'université", mimeo, ministère de l'Enseignement supérieur, Paris.

As in secondary schools, the assessment procedure serves to make the student aware of the implications of his or her choices in terms of academic requirements, commitment, and professional and social inclusion. In France, the handbook prepared for disability support services calls for a needs assessment that covers all dimensions of students' profiles, their study plan, their capacities, their centres of interest, their needs, their past difficulties, the organisation and content of the proposed course of study, the objectives to be achieved, and the methods of evaluating the course selected. The approach adopted by Aarhus University aims at teaching students to define for themselves the conditions governing their course of study by helping them initially to understand the educational options and then to identify and prioritise their centres of interest and analyse the consequences of an inappropriate choice. Trinity College Dublin holds a preliminary interview to assess support needs, at which it delivers an information document which the disability support service will review with the student, specifying their respective roles during the process, and which the student must sign in acceptance. The Limerick College of Further Education holds a preliminary meeting with students with disabilities, parents and course advisors to examine the academic record, the support and arrangements made in secondary school, and the medical or psychological certificates, and to explain to students and parents the requirements of the course and the capacities needed. The Limerick Institute of Technology helps students with disabilities recognise their strengths and weaknesses, identify the needed support and special arrangements, devise strategies, request what they need, and identify the things they can change (Figure 3.2).

This assessment procedure should make it possible to appreciate the need for support and guidance, to take the steps necessary to secure financing, and to implement the support and special arrangements the student is entitled to. It identifies the implications of the disability or specific learning problem in light of academic demands, so that appropriate arrangements can be made in terms of access to courses, adaptation of facilities, examinations or practical work assignments in a course of study, and to define the conditions of implementation. It may consider for this purpose the educational impact of the disability or the specific learning difficulty, any previous support the student may have received, and the difficulties that might appear during the university year in light of the student's profile, so that a plan can be drawn up specifying the forms of support and any measures necessary to finance them. In some cases, this plan may be transmitted to those responsible for training programmes or, when they exist, to the disability officers within each faculty for implementation. In other cases, a document specifying the authorised arrangements and support is given to the student, for the attention of teachers.

Some institutions also find it necessary to prepare the student to make use of the support or special arrangements proposed, to ensure that he or she acts with the responsibility and autonomy expected of an adult, rather than as a passive consumer. This is the case at Aarhus University, where students with dyslexia are trained to use adaptive technologies and compensatory strategies in reading and writing so that they can make better use of the arrangements offered them (Table 3.1). This is one of the objectives pursued by Montgomery College in the United States, which urges its students with disabilities to identify their strengths and weaknesses and to assert their rights and/or to be coached by a peer with tertiary education experience who can advise them on the most appropriate strategies and attitudes in light of the demands of the course and the institution.

Figure 3.2. Admission and guidance strategies of the further education programmes provided by the City of Dublin Vocational Education Committee

How the Disability and Support Service identifies and supports students

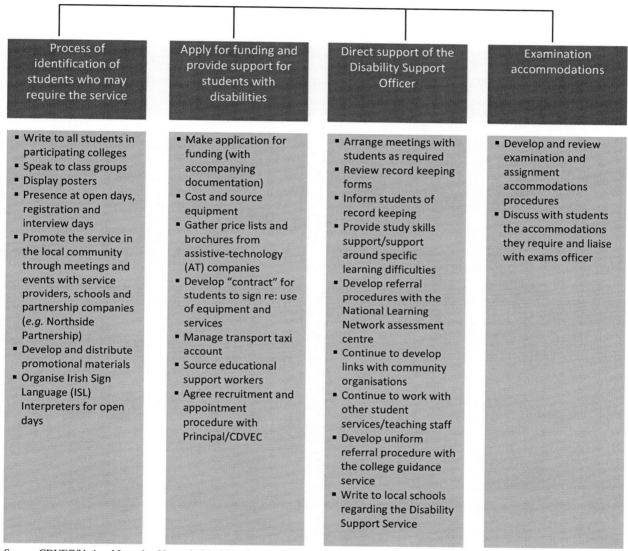

Source: CDVEC/National Learning Network, Disability Support Service, *Principals' Manual*, Dublin.

Some universities look at the conditions for implementing the plan. This may be done, as at the University of Paris 8, in the course of contacts that the disability and support services maintain with students by Internet, SMS, or specific interviews. It may also be done, as at Montgomery College, through meetings with teaching staff and students with disabilities during which adaptations needed to optimise support can be agreed.

Table 3.1. Admission procedure for dyslexic students in the University of Aarhus, Denmark

How things normally work for dyslexic students

Normal process		
Introductory session with disability service officer	Estimate the need to submit the student to dyslexia tests.	The student contacts the special education officer to discuss reading and writing problems. The service officer thinks the student may be dyslexic.
	The officer of the special education service makes an appointment for the test.	On the basis of the problems explained by the student, the officer of the special education service recommends a dyslexia test.
Test	The dyslexia test is administered by the National Agency for Education Grants and Loans (NAEGL).	In some cases the cost of the test is not covered, particularly if the NAEGL considers that the student is nearing the end of his or her studies. In these cases, NAEGL may offer a series of support sessions instead.
	The student is tested by a lexicologist at the Counselling and Support Centre.	
	Application for support proposed in the report.	The specialist normally recommends two initial series of support.
Initial support	The student learns to use the technical aid supplied in the course of these first sessions. The lexicologist reports on progress and may recommend other forms of support.	In most cases the first type of support consists of familiarisation with technical aids. In other cases the support may be pedagogical. After the initial sessions, the lexicologist generally recommends pedagogical support.
Support	The student becomes familiar with practices to compensate for reading and writing. He/she assesses his progress with the lexicologist. The lexicologist makes a progress report and may recommend further support sessions.	20-30 hours of pedagogical support are generally granted.

Source: Counselling and Support Centre, Aarhus University.

It may, more rarely, take the form of student surveys of the quality of reception and support services. For example, Trinity College Dublin and the Limerick Institute of Technology both conduct annual surveys of students with disabilities, with indicators measuring students' success, the type of activity conducted, and the number of meetings with students.

Students with disabilities have fewer chances of success in tertiary education

Access is not always synonymous with success in tertiary education. There are few data available in this area, except for those supplied by the longitudinal study of high school graduates conducted in the United States in 2000 (NLTS2), some partial surveys made by universities or countries such as Denmark, or data on the level of education of students with disabilities enrolled in tertiary education.

Existing data suggest that the path is strewn with difficulties, even failure, for a fair proportion of students with disabilities. In Denmark, they are only half as likely on average to be enrolled in the second cycle of tertiary education (Danske Studerendes Faellesrad, 2008). In the United States, they are more likely to have more non-continuous periods of study, take longer to complete courses of study or drop out at the end of the first year; only a third are likely to graduate (US General Accountability Office, 2003; Wagner *et al.*, 2006). In France, students with disabilities in university are less likely than other students to be enrolled in graduate or doctoral studies. Site visits in Denmark and

Norway indicate that students with disabilities need more time, on average, to complete their course of studies.

Transition problems in tertiary education seem particularly severe for students with a specific learning difficulty, a behavioural disorder or emotional problems (OECD, 2003). In France, for example, students with a psychological disorder, those with chronic health problems and those with a temporary disability are proportionately fewer than other students with disabilities at the graduate and doctoral levels. In Germany, students with a psychological disorder are more likely to change programme or institution and to break off their studies (Bundesministerium für Bildung und Forschung, 2007). These disparities seem, however, to have less to do with their particular circumstances than with their propensity to consider themselves disabled and to seek support. The NLTS2 study in the United States shows that while disparities in terms of impairment are not statistically significant, the propensity of students to consider themselves disabled and to ask for support differs noticeably by type of impairment. Students with an emotional disturbance, a speech problem or a specific learning difficulty are less likely than students with a motor or sensory impairment to consider themselves to have a disability, to disclose their situation, and consequently to obtain support (Newman *et al.*, 2009).

The problems of transition to tertiary education have implications for students with disabilities. They can have a financial impact, for failure or delay can be a source of indebtedness and discourage them from enrolling. They can represent a psychological burden as well, as a loss of self-confidence can be detrimental to future success, to employment and to social inclusion (Ebersold, 2007; Battle *et al.*, 1998; Rusch and Chadsey, 1998; Stodden and Jones, 2002). They require additional investments in time and energy, which can be wearing and isolate them from other students. Failing or dropping out is often a synonym of professional exclusion, a source of vulnerability and poverty. Changing course during the first semester or the first year may involve additional steps and costs that students with disabilities may be reluctant to shoulder, preferring instead to drop out. The extension of studies can be a financial burden, particularly when the student has taken out a loan and is unable to find a job and repay it. These problems perpetuate and exacerbate the inequality of access to knowledge and employment between young adults with disabilities and the general population, and thus reinforce prejudices against persons with a disability.

Co-ordinate admission and guidance strategies to build progress

The obstacles facing students with disabilities in tertiary education are greater than in secondary school, although the extent varies among institutions and faculties. Available country data suggest that access to support and special arrangements is less easy at the tertiary level. In the United States, for example, 62% of students with disabilities who left upper secondary education in 2000 were receiving support or special arrangements, whereas nearly all had received such support in the past. In a survey of Irish technology institutes conducted by AHEAD, only 50% reported that students with disabilities were fully considered in future planning, and barely two in five considered that their academic staff fully accepted responsibility for accommodating the learning needs of students with disabilities (Mulvihill, 2005). In Norway, 24% of students who participated in the "living conditions" survey had chosen a course of study other than the one they really wanted, primarily (53%) because of accessibility issues (Statistics Norway, 2007).

Improve the quality of support and special arrangements

These obstacles are attributable to the pedagogical organisation of institutions, which do not always take sufficient account of the pace of reform imposed by the Bologna process. As a result, many students with disabilities complain of growing fatigue and greater difficulties in arranging timely pedagogical adaptations. Institutions may not always pay sufficient attention to the effects of this reorientation as it may require restarting procedures, which is particularly costly in time and energy as well as financially when the cost of obtaining medical certificates is not covered. Nor do institutions always give sufficient consideration to the forward planning needs of students with disabilities: in Denmark, students complained that they were not given enough advance notice of requirements for the second semester to prepare for the necessary arrangements and to ask for the necessary pedagogical accommodation in good time.

The pedagogical organisation of institutions also does not always take sufficient account of the implications of impairment and the conditions of access to support. In Norway, some students complained of the annual bureaucratic procedures needed to obtain adaptive materials and to receive on time the necessary support and arrangements. This tends to remind them that they are students with disabilities rather than students like the others. Students with learning difficulties, unlike those with a visual problem, are not automatically eligible for adapted books and texts and thus find themselves deprived of access to course content. In Denmark, students with disabilities said they had limited access to part-time graduate studies, because only full-time students received support.

Optimise admission and support strategies

These obstacles are also attributable to the quality of admissions and support strategies, as disability support officers do not always have the skills or the tools necessary to assess students' needs accurately. In Ireland, institutes of technology do not systematically assess the needs of students with disabilities, for example, and do not always try to identify learning difficulties. The work load of the disability support services does not allow them to devote adequate time to assisting students with disabilities (Mulvihill, 2005). In Denmark, the visits showed that universities do not always assess support needs, either because they do not find it necessary or because they lack competency and do not work closely enough with the competent structures. Students interviewed pointed to the need to take more account of the evolving nature of certain pathologies and to reassess the relevant support. In Norway, students with a specific learning difficulty or a psychological disorder said they are hampered in their coursework by problems for combining their studies with the various activities of daily life, while students with a mobility impairment and those with respiratory problems are more inclined than others to have trouble completing their course (Bjerkan *et al.*, 2009). Some American students interviewed were concerned that "self-advocacy" initiatives were not enough to overcome problems arising from differences in approaches to disability and the lack of co-operation among professionals. More generally, admissions strategies may have difficulty encouraging students with disabilities to become independent and/or empowering them to take an active part in implementing support and accommodations. This may be particularly true if admissions strategies give priority to pedagogical issues to the detriment of those favouring students' inclusion into the university community.

Moreover, the pedagogical support available does not always have the required quality. It may be difficult to mobilise university personnel to improve pedagogical accessibility, and teachers may be reluctant to offer pedagogical accommodation, especially for students whose problems are invisible (*e.g.* specific learning difficulties or psychological disorders). Students interviewed generally wanted information on the range and quality of available support and accommodation, so as not to have to find this out as they go. Some students in Ireland asked for easier access to computer rooms, to technological aids and to better software. Students with a sight problem complained that books and methodological supports arrived late, limiting their ability to keep up with their coursework and thus jeopardising their academic success as well as their inclusion into the university community. Students with a sensory problem may complain that sign language interpreters are not sufficiently skilled or are not always available to help them keep up with other students in their classes.

Students with a chronic illness or a psychological disorder may feel that the accelerated pace of the Bologna reforms has increased their level of fatigue and that the increasing use of group work deprives them of some arrangements since they have to keep pace with the other students. In the United States, 10.2% of students with disabilities drop out of education for reasons of health or time (Newman *et al.*, 2009).

Special examination arrangements are not always of the required quality. Faculties may be reluctant to give students with a chronic illness the right to special accommodation. Dyslexia or allergies may be known too late to accommodate the facilities, especially when special rooms have to be reserved well in advance. A lack of co-ordination between the examinations body and the disability support service can be a source of misunderstanding. Students with disabilities may not have access to the planned arrangements or the conditions may be unsatisfactory. Institutions such as George Washington University, provide students with disabilities with a model letter and encourage them to write to their professors with details about their impairment or specific learning difficulty and the accommodation they will need.

Encourage integration in the university community

These obstacles are also attributable to the isolation felt by some students with disabilities, which can lead to failure and, according to some students, constitutes a heavy psychological burden. Danish students complained that adapted transport was available only on the direct route between home and school, so that they were unable to participate in off-campus activities that would facilitate their social inclusion. The lack of texts in Braille or appropriate teaching aids significantly increases the workload of students with visual impairments and specific learning difficulties, makes it harder for them to combine work and study, and isolates them from their fellow students. Since the costs of sign language interpretation are covered only during teaching hours, deaf students or those with hearing problems may have trouble communicating with other students outside the classroom and find themselves progressively isolated. Students with a mobility impairment are affected by the lack of physical accessibility, which may impede their mobility on campus, require a great deal of extra time, and prevent them from participating in all planned curricular activities (*e.g.* group work), again a source of isolation.

These difficulties are a reminder that the quality of the transition to tertiary education depends on linking admission and guidance in order to ensure the independence and empowerment of students with disabilities as well as the quality of the support and special arrangements provided throughout the process. The Limerick Institute of Technology (LIT) offers an example of a particularly interesting innovation. It provides tutors to new students during the first weeks of the academic year. This facilitates the identification of persons with difficulties, steers them to the necessary support and accommodation services, and helps to implement solutions. Interviews revealed other initiatives that, like those taken by George Washington University, encourage teachers to inform new students about the disability support services available or to alert those services to persons who may have a specific learning difficulty (Table 3.2). They also stressed the importance of measure that, like the learning support laboratory of Montgomery College, can help students with disabilities in areas in which they encounter difficulties.

Table 3.2. Information provided to students with disabilities and to staff

Ten things that students and faculties need to know about the disability support service for students with special education needs		
	Students with disabilities	Faculty
1. Interaction	Students should present themselves during the first two weeks of term.	The University should encourage disabilities to be reported and noted promptly, upon registration.
2. Guidance	Students should meet regularly with their professors for assistance and advice in their work.	The University is the greatest resource for students and should work with them closely.
3. Confidentiality	Students have the right to absolute confidentiality *vis-à-vis* their peers and faculty.	The University must never disclose a student's disability, of whatever kind.
4. Eligibility	Students must provide the usual certificates to be entitled to assistance.	The University should steer students to the Disability Service if they are not registered with it.
5. Adaptation	Students may have access to a series of adaptive accommodation programmes.	University has a legal obligation to make the adaptations recommended by the Disability Service.
6. Examinations	Students are often entitled to more time, depending on the nature of their disability.	The University must recognise that students may not have unlimited time for examinations.
7. Note taking	Students are often entitled to help of a peer note taker, depending on the nature of their disability.	The University should co-operate by seeking the assistance of student note takers at the beginning of the semester.
8. Rights	Students have rights guaranteed by federal law.	The University should keep abreast of regulations concerning persons with disabilities.
9. Complaints	Students must first try to resolve any conflicts with their professors.	The University should contact the Disability Service when mediation is necessary or desirable.
10. Advocacy	The disability support services must encourage students to ask questions about support.	The Disability Service must encourage university staff to advise it of any concerns.

Source: George Washington University (Washington, DC).

Create an inclusive ethos favourable to the integration and success of students with disabilities

It is not always easy to link admissions and guidance strategies. Admissions strategies may be confined to distributing information, particularly when the staff in charge are not sufficiently trained and equipped or when disability support services are not co-ordinated with other units or faculties. Support plans may be designed for administrative convenience and seek to inform students rather than develop guidance that mobilises all actors around common objectives. This may particularly be the case when budgets do not reflect the growing number of students with disabilities, when disability support staff feel isolated from the university community or are not able to devote the time required to identify needs and work with students (Brandt, 2005).

Mobilise the entire university community around the success of every student

Beyond the mobilisation of technical, financial and human resources, the quality of transition is intimately linked to the presence of an inclusive ethos, in which openness to disability and accessibility is a component of the institutional culture respected by all. Aarhus University is committed to ensuring that all students who meet admission requirements, including those with disabilities, can achieve their potential and satisfy the academic requirements of their chosen course of study, provided they commit themselves actively to their own success. Trinity College Dublin outlines its accessibility policy in documents that are available via the Internet and in handbooks prepared for this purpose, and it has developed a strategy for diversity that extends not only to student admissions and support but also to the training of staff, so that disability is a matter of concern to the entire university community.

An inclusive ethos calls for mobilising the entire university community around the success of each student, including those with a disability or specific learning difficulty. Mobilisation can be achieved by resource persons who make known the work done by the disability support service so as to ensure continuity and coherence of support and accommodations. The institutional policy of Oslo University calls for each faculty to appoint a disability officer to support the work of the disability support service, to ensure implementation of the support and special arrangements to which students with disabilities are entitled, and to see to their quality. Aarhus University's policy makes needs assessment the responsibility of the person designated within each faculty to receive students; this person is expected to take the administrative steps necessary to finance the assessment procedure, and to request the guidance and support centre to perform tests and identify any support and special arrangements needed. The accessibility plan of Trinity College Dublin designates liaison personnel within each faculty to serve as advisors for students with disabilities and their teachers, to make faculty members aware of accessibility, to speak for teachers, and to suggest curricular reforms to make faculties pedagogically more accessible.

This mobilisation requires raising the university community's awareness of the driving role of diversity in terms of innovation and creativity, of the adverse effect of prejudices against students with disabilities (particularly those whose disability is not visible) and of the role that every person has to play in integrating these students into the institution. Awareness raising can be accomplished through information sessions dealing with disability to familiarise the university community with institutional policy, the support available to students and its financing, and the missions and activities of the disability support services. Awareness may also be enhanced through handbooks and tools targeted at the teaching body to encourage them not to identify students solely in terms of their disability, to alert the disability support services to students experiencing serious difficulties, and to change attitudes and teaching practices with respect to these students. Handbooks can provide information on the educational implications of impairment and learning difficulties, on strategies for encouraging students to disclose their particular education needs, on ways of discussing matters with them candidly, and on pedagogical accommodations that can render courses accessible to all students regardless of their particular circumstances.

Mobilisation also requires training for implementing an inclusive curriculum. Universities may develop special training programmes for their teaching staff, such as those of the disability support service of George Washington University or the publications provided to the faculty by the HEATH programme. Training can also be provided as part of the institutional accessibility policy, along the lines of the three-day training that Trinity College Dublin gives all new teachers to inform them of the institution's policy and to make them aware of the diversity of educational profiles in a given class and the tools and teaching methods they can use to respond to different educational needs. Training may also aim to generalise inclusive practices in all components of the institution and may take the form of manuals, teaching tools or self-evaluation tools that encourage teachers to be pedagogically innovative and create a teaching environment accessible to all students, and to adopt knowledge assessment methods that allow students to progress to the best of their ability.

Mobilisation can also be organised around role models that are meaningful to students with disabilities. Institutions such as Oslo University may ask students with an exemplary record despite a disability or a specific learning difficulty to serve as mentors to new students and share their experience, help them to integrate the university community, make them aware of their aptitudes, and help them define and achieve their academic, professional and personal goals. For its part, George Washington University has created a website as well as videos and CDs so that students with disabilities can learn about personal, academic and professional success stories.

This mobilisation can also be achieved through teaching programmes specifically devoted to students with a disability or a specific learning difficulty. A number of American universities and a few European ones (for example Trinity College Dublin in partnership with Cork University) have developed initiatives of this kind. Such training can help to open doors to tertiary education for young adults with disabilities and enhance the inclusiveness of institutions by promoting links between students with disabilities and other students, encouraging teachers to make their teaching more accessible and making disability an integral component of diversity.

Develop an educational approach to disability

Mobilisation relies on the efforts of the disability support services to reach out to the university community and encourage it to accept disability, to change the way it sees students with disabilities, and to modify its practices. As Montgomery College insists, accessibility must empower students to pursue strategies and attitudes to optimise their chances for success and prepare them to be responsible citizens and leaders, open to learning throughout their lives.

This work depends however on the approach suggested by the definition of disability retained. The inclusive ethos is particularly present, to varying degrees among institutions, in Denmark, Ireland, Norway and the United States. These countries have adopted an educational approach to disability that relates it to the educational needs inherent in the diversity of student profiles to which institutions must respond rather than to an inability. In these countries, as indicated earlier, the majority of students with disabilities have a specific learning difficulty.

According to this approach, the diversity of educational profiles is a source of success and development for the entire university community and disability is an element of its diversity. Accessibility is related to the educational needs of the entire student body, rather than to the specific characteristics of those with a disability. George Washington

University insists that students with disabilities, like all students, must contribute to the well-being and development of the university community. In the United States, Montgomery College (Maryland) is committed to equal opportunity and to ensuring the success of all students, including those with disabilities, while the support and special arrangements provided by the University of Copenhagen to students with disabilities are, by law, included in the services offered to all students. Trinity College Dublin has responded to the diversification of the student body – one component of which is disability – with a project to empower teachers across the entire institution to develop an inclusive curriculum. In fact, 19% of students with disabilities admitted in 2008 benefited from support programmes other than those specifically for students with disabilities.

Institutional policies seek, therefore, to combine the implementation of a universal design for learning environment involving the whole university community with the allocation of support and accommodation for students with special educational needs. The University of Oslo has established a teaching environment committee to examine the institution's accessibility and issue recommendations for creating a pedagogical environment accessible to all students, in observance of the "universal design for learning" principle. The disability support service of Aarhus University is an integral part of the institution and the information on its website is directed towards staff as well as students with disabilities. George Washington University defines "universal design for learning" as a method for designing a curriculum that can adapt to the variety of educational needs and learning styles and create learning experiences that suit the learner and maximise his or her ability to progress. Montgomery College's policy states that everyone in the institution has to provide curricular accommodations and to support students with disabilities and it is therefore an instrument to favour the inclusion of the entire community.

The educational approach to disability leads tertiary education institutions to consider support and accommodation as a source of development for the entire institution. The University of Copenhagen does not develop specific programmes for students with disabilities since the institution should be accessible to all, including students with specific educational needs. For Trinity College Dublin, pedagogical accessibility is beneficial to all students, and not only to "atypical" students, *e.g.* those with specific learning needs, foreign students, or students from disadvantaged backgrounds. Montgomery College and the University of Copenhagen both offer counselling to all students for managing stress and conflicts, or any other factor that could jeopardise their success.

An accessibility policy is not restricted to the institution but also extends to its environment. The Limerick Institute of Technology sees itself as playing a pivotal role in the social and cultural development of its region and creates partnerships, establishes new ties with its environment, and takes initiatives that will enhance access to tertiary education for disadvantaged groups. Institutions are adopting piloting tools for planning and optimising their accessibility policy, as Trinity College Dublin has done.

This inclusive ethos is less prevalent in countries that still take a diagnostic approach to disability, which emphasises students' educability and/or relies on more or less strict anti-discrimination legislation. That view is still predominant in the Czech Republic and to a lesser extent in France where it has receded following the law of 11 February 2005. In these countries, as indicated earlier, students with disabilities have mainly a sensory or motor impairment or a health problem.

While the situation may vary from one institution to the next, universities in these countries tend to view diversity as an exception for exceptional students. They see the disability issue as being of secondary importance. It engages the institution's collective responsibility only moderately and depends on the initiative of individuals rather than on mobilising the university community as a whole.

The presence of students with disabilities is seen as a constraint that can hamper the institution's proper functioning. The admission and academic progress of these students are viewed as issues of concern to a minority. The accessibility issue is rarely explicitly addressed in any policy or plan of action involving all of the institution's staff. Staff responsible for support and guidance may play only a marginal role, and advisors designated to manage support and guidance at faculty level may be unwilling to do so. The link between faculties and disability support services may therefore be tenuous, and the support and special arrangements provided will not always have the desired quality.

Support and special arrangements are geared primarily to resolving problems associated with students' deficiencies rather than addressing the issue of equity in order to put every student on the path to success. Admission and support of students with disabilities do not often result from a collective commitment at institutional level but from individual efforts and conviction and the influence of the disability support services' staff. Tertiary education institutions may not have a specific service for the reception of students with disabilities and may entrust this task to members of the university community who may not have the qualifications or the time to perform it properly. The resources mobilised may fall short of requirements, as many interviewees noted. Teachers may be reluctant to make special arrangements, particularly if they are inadequately informed about the various aspects and facets of impairments and about the teaching practices that they could use to help students with disabilities to overcome their difficulties.

Secondary and tertiary education institutions need more support

Despite the progress made, schools and universities still face difficulties, to varying degrees, for ensuring the continuity and coherence of students' itinerary beyond secondary education. The road to tertiary education for young adults with disabilities is often uneven and marked by problems of adaptation, and their progress in tertiary education often requires an investment of time and energy that prolongs the length of studies and can be a source of isolation and failure.

These difficulties arise because upper secondary schools do not make transition an integral component of their policy and are insufficiently integrated into their environment to mobilise the resources needed to support students with disabilities and equip the staff responsible for transition. They also reflect strategies for preparing upper secondary students that pay much more attention to informing students than to accompanying them throughout the transition process. They may therefore overlook the special needs associated with an impairment or a specific learning difficulty and fail to empower secondary school students to meet the requirements of tertiary education and to take charge of their future.

These difficulties also arise because tertiary education institutions fail to make disability a component of their policy or to promote an inclusive ethos that mobilises the entire community around the success and future of each student, including those with a disability. They also reflect the impact of admissions strategies that do not link the admission of students with disabilities to guidance throughout their studies in order to empower them and to integrate them into the university community. These difficulties are exacerbated when universities are inadequately integrated into their environment, when their disability support services are isolated from other student services and from other services for young adults with disabilities, and when the coherence of student admissions and support is left largely to the initiative of the staff member involved.

The reluctance of institutions to make disability a component of their institutional policy and to promote an inclusive ethos is all the more important because the methodological incentives described in the previous chapter do not always suffice to mobilise institutions to include students with disabilities. The methodological supports offered are less well developed (although they are improving) than those provided in secondary schools, and support networks are unable to respond fully to the needs of disability support service staff and to the questions they face on a daily basis.

Training in the university community is also less developed than in secondary schools and only Denmark, Ireland and the United States reported providing such training. According to the country report, Denmark has earmarked DKK 4 billion (EUR 500 000) to 2012 for improving the quality of tertiary education and strengthening teaching skills: 3% of the budget (EUR 20 million) is allocated to teachers of short- and medium-term cycles of tertiary education over the period 2007-09, and 5.5% (EUR 30 million) to teaching methods and teacher training in the long cycles offered by universities. In Ireland, the Dublin Centre for Academic Development has since 2009 offered professional development courses for teachers. In the United States, the Department of Education provides financial support to tertiary institutions that offer training to upgrade the quality of teaching.

Few countries reported any training for staff of disability support services. These may therefore be inadequately trained and equipped to do their job. Where it exists, such training is often provided through existing support networks, such as the sessions organised in France by the Ministry of Tertiary Education and Research, or the meetings organised in Ireland by the Disability Advisors Working Network. Particularly interesting in this regard is the training provided by Aarhus University in Denmark for admission and support staff in the region, as well as that offered by George Washington University.

Conclusion

The continuity and coherence of students' itineraries beyond secondary education depend on strategies developed by upper secondary and tertiary education institutions. The work performed by upper secondary schools to prepare young adults with disabilities can allow them to adapt opportunities to their expectations and needs and guide them throughout the transition process, while admissions strategies in tertiary education can facilitate their access and success.

Upper secondary schools' strategies aim to provide young adults with disabilities with information and advice to help them to make choices that are appropriate to their possibilities and professional wishes. They encourage them in addition to plan carefully and as early as possible the different steps of the transition process to tertiary education as well as the means required. They prepare them more rarely to face the requirements they may encounter after secondary education and are not always able to offer guidance during the transition process. Young adults with disabilities may feel isolated when leaving upper secondary schools, may encounter hurdles due to administrative procedures or find frustrating a lack of information on the level of accessibility of tertiary education institutions.

Admissions strategies at tertiary education level aim at helping students with disabilities to become actively involved in their programme of studies and at ensuring that the institution mobilises the means required for their success. They aim at preventing risks of failure by involving stakeholders responsible for extracurricular issues or by encouraging the involvement of families. They work to encourage students to be responsible for themselves by developing an action plan which describes the support and accommodations provided and by forging a contractual relationship between the student and the institution. Admissions strategies seek more rarely to combine admissions and guidance strategies or to develop guidance methodologies aiming at students' empowerment and autonomy. This may lessen the quality of support and accommodation, and students with disabilities may have difficulty meeting academic requirements and become isolated from the university community. As a result, their opportunities to progress will be lower than those of their non-disabled peers.

In sum, for students with disabilities, access to and success in tertiary education not only requires information, additional resources or specific arrangements. It also requires the development at institutional level of an inclusive ethos that makes of diversity an added value for the entire university community and universal design for learning a cultural dimension of the institution.

References

Battle, D., L. Dickens-Wright and S. Murphy (1998), "How to Empower Adolescents: Guidelines for Effective Self-advocacy", *Teaching Exceptional Children,* Vol. 30(3), pp. 28-33.

Bjerkan, K.Y. and M. Veenstra (2008), Utdanning, arbeid, bolig og transport for unge voksne 20 til 35 år. In *Statusrapport 08: samfunnsutviklingen for personer med nedsatt funksjonsevne*, Nasjonalt dokumentasjonssenter for personer med nedsatt funksjonsevne, Oslo, pp. 154-207.

Bjerkan, K.Y., M. Veenstra and J. Eriksen (2009), "Levekårene blant unge voksne: bedring, men godt nok?", Paper presented at the Konferanse om levekårene for personer med nedsatt funksjonsevne.

Brandt, S.S. (2005), *Høyere utdanning - tilgjengelig for alle?: studenter med funksjonsnedsettelse og funksjonshemning i høyere utdanning - Kvalitetsreformens betydning og lærestedenes strategier for inkludering*, No. 4/2005, NIFU STEP, Oslo.

Bundesministerium für Bildung und Forschung (2007), *Die wirtschaftliche und soziale Lage der Studierenden in der Bundesrepublik Deutschland 2006*; 18. Sozialerhebung des Deutschen Studentenwerks durchgeführt durch HIS Hochschul-Informations-System, Bonn/Berlin.

Cameto, R., P. Levine and M. Wagner (2004), *Transition Planning for Students with Disabilities. A Special Topic Report from the National Longitudinal Transition Study-2 (NLTS2)*, SRI International, Menlo Park, CA.

Conférence des Présidents d'Université (2007), "Guide de l'accueil de l'étudiant handicapé à l'université", mimeo, ministère de l'Enseignement supérieur, Paris

Danske Studerendes Faellesrad (2008), *Vi er jo ikk en del af universitetets bevidstehd... en undersogelse af barrierer for studerende med handicap npa de lange videregaende uddannelser.* Report Danske Studerendes Faellesrad, Copenhagen.

Ebersold, S. (2005), *Le temps des servitudes. La famille à l'épreuve du handicap*, PUR, Rennes.

Ebersold, S. (2007), "Affiliating Participation for an Active Citizenship", *Scandinavian Journal of Disability Research*, Vol. 9 (3).

Ebersold, S. (2008), "Adapting Higher Education to the Needs of Disabled Students: Developments, Challenges and Prospects", in OECD, *Higher Education to 2030, Volume 1: Demography*, OECD, Paris.

Mulvihill, R. (2005), *Participation of and Services for Students with Disabilities in Institutes of Technology*, AHEAD.

Newman, L. *et al.* (2009), *The Post-High School Outcomes of Youth with Disabilities up to 4 Years After High School,* SRI International, Menlo Park, CA.

OECD (2003), *Disability in Higher Education*, OECD, Paris.

Rusch, F.R. and J.G. Chadsey (eds.) (1998), *Beyond High School: Transition from School to Work,* Wadsworth, Belmont, CA.

Statistics Norway (2007), *Ungdoms levekår, Tor Morten Normann (red.),* Statistisk sentralbyrå, Oslo.

Stodden, R.A. and M.A. Jones (2002), *Supporting Youth with Disabilities to Access and Succeed in Postsecondary Education: Essentials for Educators in Secondary Schools,* National Center on Secondary Education and Transition Issue Brief, 1(5), University of Minnesota, Minneapolis,MN.

US General Accountability Office (2003), *College Completion: Additional Efforts could Help Education with its Completion Goal, GAO-03-568*, GPO, Washington, DC.

Wagner, M. *et al.* (2005), *After High School: A First Look at the Postschool Experiences of Youth with Disabilities, A report from the National Longitudinal Transition Study-2 (NLTS2)*, SRI International, Menlo Park, CA.

Wagner, M. *et al.* (2006), *An Overview of Findings From Wave 2 of the National Longitudinal Transition Study-2 (NLTS2)*, SRI International, Menlo Park, CA.

Chapter 4

The difficult transition from education to employment

The growing number of young adults with disabilities in tertiary education has had only a relative impact in terms of entry into employment. Young adults with disabilities have less straightforward access to employment than the population as a whole, are overexposed to long-term unemployment and to casual or part-time jobs, and, as a result, to poverty. In this respect, their transition to employment requires the strengthening of links between schools and the job market as well as the development of synergies to combine success in tertiary education with successful entry into society and employment. It is important to facilitate the acquisition of professional experience in tertiary education, to make better provision for employment in the strategies of admissions and support services for students with disabilities and to strengthen the links between tertiary education institutions and the world of work.

Introduction

This chapter looks at access to employment after leaving secondary school and, more particularly, following graduation from tertiary education. It does not attempt an exhaustive description of the employment situation of young adults with disabilities – such an undertaking deserves a specific study, such as the one conducted by the OECD Directorate for Employment, Labour and Social Affairs on employment opportunities for persons with disabilities in Denmark, Ireland and Norway, or on jobs for youth (OECD, 2006, 2008a, 2009b, 2009c, 2010). It seeks, rather, to determine the extent to which secondary and tertiary education addresses the question of employment so as to ensure that young adults with disabilities who cannot pursue tertiary education will not find themselves excluded from the labour market, to allow those who wish to pursue an occupational activity during their studies to do so and find employment thereafter, and to facilitate access to employment upon completion of tertiary education.

Once again, the data described in the country reports on the employment of young adults with disabilities does not provide a very clear picture. With the exception of the United States, existing data do not allow for determining the specific situation of young adults with disabilities leaving secondary education. Nor can they be used, for the most part, to compare their situation with that of the young adult population as a whole. They do not give precise information on discrimination against young adults with disabilities in terms of employment and its impact in terms of vulnerability and exclusion. Existing published data are rarely sufficient to identify the 18-25 year age group most concerned by the transition to tertiary education. For example, in the United States, while data on disabled recipients of supplemental security income (SSI) allow for breakdowns by age and average monthly earnings, those on employment do not allow for specifying the situation of young adults with disabilities among the working-age population (18-64 years), although it may in fact differ from that of older adults with disabilities. In addition, employment statistics published by the American Community Survey (ACS) or the Current Population Survey (CPS) do not provide breakdowns by age.

Better access to mainstream education but limited employment impact

Access to employment is more difficult than for the general population

While the growing presence of young adults with disabilities in tertiary education brings their level of training closer to the average of young adults in certain countries, this seems to have a relatively minor impact on their access to employment (Berthoud, 2006). In Ireland, economic growth was unable to reverse the decline in the employment rate for persons with disabilities, which dropped by 3% between 2002 and 2004, particularly for those with sight problems. In France, their employment rate fell by 1% between 2002 and 2007, when the population without disabilities rose by 3% (Nguyen and Ulrich, 2008). In Norway, the employment rate of persons with disabilities rose less than that of the active population as a whole. In addition the employment rate of holders of tertiary education degrees fell by 10% between 2005 and 2008, while that of the general population rose by 7% (Statistics Norway, 2009). The number of persons with disabilities exiting the labour market in the Czech Republic rose sharply between 2002 and 2008, while the number of persons working or unemployed virtually stagnated (Ministry of Education of the Czech Republic, 2009).

Access to employment is particularly difficult for older persons with disabilities (OECD, 2006, 2008a). In France between 2003 and 2006, for instance, the number of job seekers with disabilities increased for the older generations but decreased by 19% for job seekers with disabilities under the age of 25, to 3.9% (Nguyen and Ulrich, 2008). Nonetheless, young adults with disabilities still face greater obstacles for employment than the average of young adults. As Figure 4.1 indicates, their employment rate is well below that of their age group as a whole in all countries. The difference is greatest in the Czech Republic (-44%), in Ireland (-25%) and in Norway (-18.8%) but less marked in Denmark (-8%) and France (-5%).

Figure 4.1. Employment rates for young adults with disabilities (20-30 year-olds)

In selected OECD countries (%)

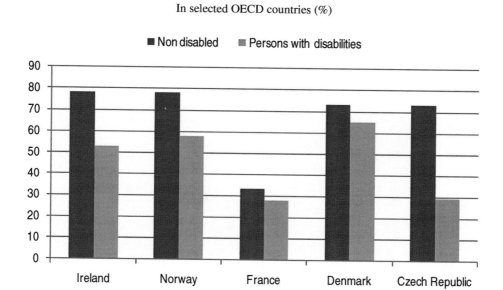

Source: Czech Republic: Ministry of Education of the Czech Republic (2009), "Transitions to Tertiary Education and to Employment for Young People with Impairments and Learning Difficulties", Country background report, Prague; France: Délégation ministérielle à l'emploi des personnes handicapées (2009), "Parcours des personnes handicapées vers l'enseignement supérieur et vers l'emploi", Country background report, ministère de l'Éducation nationale, Paris; Norway: OECD (2006), *Sickness, Disability and Work: Breaking the Barriers, Volume 1: Norway, Poland and Switzerland*, OECD, Paris; Denmark and Ireland: OECD (2008a), *Sickness, Disability and Work: Breaking the Barriers, Volume 3: Denmark, Finland, Ireland and the Netherlands*, OECD, Paris.

Difficulties for entering employment depend on the severity of the disability (OECD, 2003). In the United States, for example, young persons with a mobility impairment, a cognitive impairment, or an emotional disturbance are less likely to obtain employment after secondary school than those with a health problem or learning difficulties (Wagner *et al.*, 2005). In Norway, young adults are least likely to be employed if they consider themselves to be in poor health, and especially if they have a sensory, respiratory or cognitive disability (Bjerkan and Veenstra, 2008). In France, persons aged 20-29 with a mobility impairment, a cognitive impairment or a psychological disorder are more likely to be unemployed than those with a visceral or metabolic impairment or a sensory impairment (Amar and Samira, 2003).

Greater risk of unemployment

These difficulties in obtaining employment mean that young adults with disabilities are more likely to be unemployed. Their unemployment rate is twice the average in Ireland. It is 2% above the average in the Czech Republic and 3% above the average in Denmark (Figure 4.2).

Figure 4.2. Unemployment rate for young adults with disabilities (20-30 year-olds)

In selected OECD countries (%)

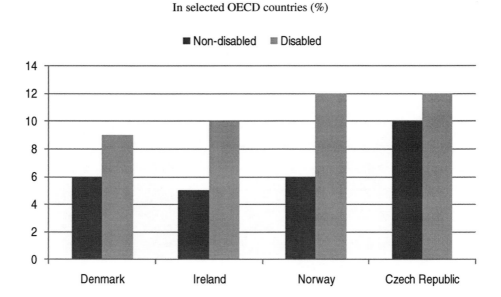

Source: Czech Republic: Ministry of Education of the Czech Republic (2009), "Transitions to Tertiary Education and to Employment for Young People with Impairments and Learning Difficulties", Country background report, Prague; Norway: OECD (2006), *Sickness, Disability and Work: Breaking the Barriers, Volume 1: Norway, Poland and Switzerland*, OECD, Paris; Denmark and Ireland: OECD (2008a), *Sickness, Disability and Work: Breaking the Barriers, Volume 3: Denmark, Finland, Ireland and the Netherlands*, OECD, Paris.

In the United States, the unemployment rate for persons with disabilities aged 16-64 in 2009 was 14.5% versus 9.0% for the general population (Disabled World, 2010; US Department of Labor, 2010).

Greater risk of exclusion

In addition, difficulties for entering employment overexpose young adults with disabilities to definitive exclusion from the labour market. In Norway, despite government efforts, the proportion of young adults receiving sickness or disability allowances six years after leaving school is nearly twice the rate for young persons with disabilities who are unemployed or receiving support from active labour market programmes (OECD, 2006). In Denmark, despite the rising employment rate for persons with disabilities, the number of benefit recipients with disabilities aged 20-34 rose by nearly 10% between 1995 and 2006 (OECD, 2008a).

Table 4.1. Activity status of persons aged 15-29 in the Czech Republic (2007)

	Status	Numbers (thousands)	%
Total population	Employed	924.1	43.8
	Unemployed	110.2	5.2
	Inactive	1076.6	51.0
Young adults with disabilities	Employed	8.3	22.3
	Unemployed	2.9	7.8
	Inactive	26.0	70.0

Source: Ministry of Education of the Czech Republic, "Transitions to Tertiary Education and to Employment for Young People with Impairments and Learning Difficulties", Country background report, Ministry of Education of the Czech Republic, Prague.

In Ireland, 7% of persons with disabilities aged 15-24 are neither in employment nor in education (NEET); the equivalent figure for those without disabilities in that age group is 3% (Central Statistical Office, 2009). Moreover, 20.4% of persons aged 20-24 have withdrawn from the labour market because of a disability (OECD, 2008a). In the Czech Republic, 70% of young adults with disabilities aged 15-29 are inactive, versus 51% in that age group among the general population (Ministry of Education of the Czech Republic, 2009).

Employment opportunities are often temporary and part-time

When young adults with disabilities have access to employment, they are more likely to have temporary jobs. These may not give them professionally marketable experience and may overexpose them to recurrent unemployment. In the United States, 56% of young adults with disabilities who were working in 2008 had been in employment for less than 10 months, versus 15 months for the general population. Young adults with disabilities in the most unstable employment situations had emotional disturbances (having held 3.4 jobs on average since leaving high school), had learning difficulties (2.9 jobs), an intellectual disability (2.1 jobs), or a mobility impairment (1.6 jobs) (Newman *et al.*, 2009). As Figure 4.3 indicates, young Norwegians and Danes with disabilities are more likely to have a temporary job, while in Ireland the proportion is very close to that for young adults as a whole.

Young adults with disabilities are also more likely than the average to be working part-time and may therefore have fewer financial resources and, in some countries, a lower level of social protection. The French country report indicates that more than 50% of employees with disabilities on a fixed-term contract were working part-time in 2005. As Figure 4.4 shows, young adults with disabilities are more likely to hold part-time jobs than the general population in Denmark (+7%), in Ireland (+6%) and in Norway (although, at +3%, the gap is smaller) (OECD, 2006, 2008a).

The majority of American students with disabilities surveyed by the National Transition Longitudinal Study-2 (NLTS2) were working full-time. The proportion was largest among those with a learning difficulty, other health problems and speech language impairments. Two-thirds of those working part-time said they wanted to do so (Newman *et al.*, 2009).

Figure 4.3. Exposure to temporary employment among young adults with and without disabilities[1]

In certain countries participating in the project (%)

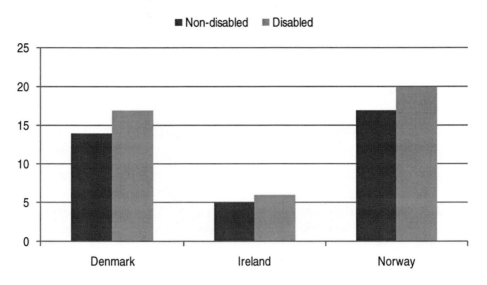

1. Latest available year.

Source: OECD (2006), *Sickness, Disability and Work: Breaking the Barriers, Volume 1: Norway, Poland and Switzerland*, OECD, Paris; OECD (2008), *Sickness, Disability and Work: Breaking the Barriers, Volume 3: Denmark, Finland, Ireland and the Netherlands*, OECD, Paris.

Figure 4.4. Part-time employment of young adults with and without disabilities

In certain countries participating in the project (%)

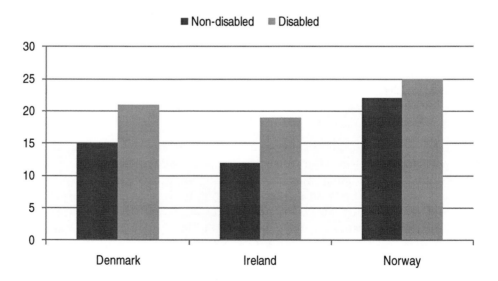

Source: OECD (2006), *Sickness, Disability and Work: Breaking the Barriers, Volume 1: Norway, Poland and Switzerland*, OECD, Paris; OECD (2008a), *Sickness, Disability and Work: Breaking the Barriers, Volume 3: Denmark, Finland, Ireland and the Netherlands*, OECD, Paris.

As shown in Figure 4.5, young adults with disabilities are more likely than young adults without disabilities to be employed in the services sector, except in Norway. In Denmark, for example, 75% of young adults with disabilities work in this sector, versus 73% of the general population. The comparable figures for Ireland are 68% and 65%.

Figure 4.5. Employment of young adults, by sector

In certain countries participating in the project (%)

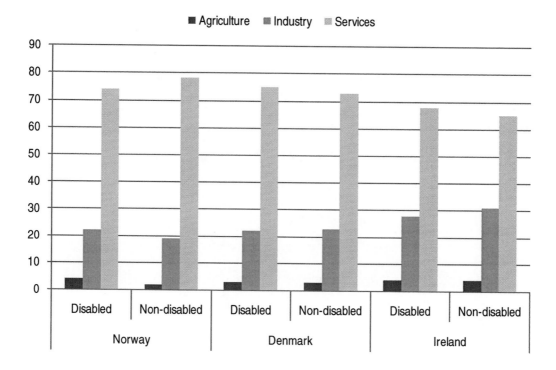

Source: OECD (2006), *Sickness, Disability and Work: Breaking the Barriers, Volume 1: Norway, Poland and Switzerland*, OECD, Paris; OECD (2008a), *Sickness, Disability and Work: Breaking the Barriers, Volume 3: Denmark, Finland, Ireland and the Netherlands*, OECD, Paris.

This is also the case in the United States, where young adults with disabilities interviewed during the NLTS2 Wave 3 are more likely to work in food services than in most other types of jobs (Newman *et al.*, 2009).

Strengthening linkages between upper secondary school and the labour market

These difficulties are closely related to shifting labour market patterns. The decline in unskilled jobs is a disadvantage for young adults with a cognitive impairment, and the growing importance attached by recruiters to behavioural characteristics makes it more difficult for persons with a behavioural or psychological disorder to find work (OECD, 2003).

These difficulties also relate to the ability of the education system to prepare young adults with disabilities to meet the demands of the labour market. Among those who wish to work following secondary school, employers have difficulty finding qualified persons with disabilities, especially among the young (Wagner *et al.*, 2005; Powell *et al.*, 2008).

Access to vocational education and training or to education programmes which include a career component plays an essential role in a context in which a diploma is increasingly important but less and less sufficient for obtaining employment (OECD, 2008b, 2009a). Such courses improve access to knowledge and behavioural skills required, for example, for teamwork, and convey useful work experience for the transition to work.

Transition to employment at the end of secondary education seems in this respect to be easier in Norway and in Denmark than in other countries (OECD, 2008c, 2010). As Figure 4.6 shows, upper secondary education in Norway includes more ISCED 3B and 3C courses than the OECD average, and the education authorities consult employers about the curriculum, the content of vocational education and training courses, the skills required and the forms of certification awarded (OECD, 2009a). While Denmark offers relatively fewer ISCED 3B and 3C courses than Norway, links with the employment sector are closer, as the authorities involve employers in defining the training courses offered and the work-school combination (dual system) is more frequent in education programmes (OECD, 2010).

Figure 4.6. Students enrolled in public and private upper secondary education

By type of programme

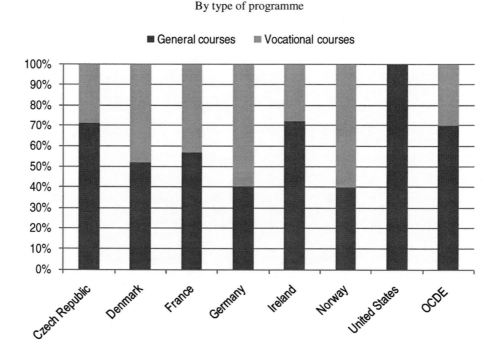

Source: OECD (2009), *Education at a Glance*, OECD, Paris.

Ireland, the Czech Republic and, to a lesser extent, France offer fewer vocational training opportunities in upper secondary education than the OECD average. While school-work combinations are becoming more available, they are still very rare in Ireland (3% of secondary students) and in France (12%), compared to nearly 50% in Denmark and about 20% in Norway (OECD, 2008c). In the Czech Republic, social partners are not always consulted on vocational education and training issues (Kuczera, 2010). In Ireland, upper secondary students with disabilities enrolled in vocational training courses can follow the leaving certificate vocational programme which leads to tertiary education, or the leaving certificate applied, which gives eligibility for further education programmes but not tertiary education. In France, vocational education and training is offered in professional upper secondary schools as part of a course that includes a practical working assignment in a firm and can lead to tertiary education; it can also be provided in regional institutions of adapted education (*établissements régionaux d'enseignements adaptés* – EREA) which are often dedicated to a type of disability and combine schooling with medical and paramedical support.

In the United States, career and technical education (CTE) is concentrated at the tertiary level, although secondary school programmes increasingly offer work-related courses as an integral part of the high-school curriculum. Most states have now developed high school programmes that combine general academic subjects with CTE courses, with clearly defined pedagogical and professional objectives. Missouri, for instance, has programmes in which secondary, tertiary and CTE instructors are all expected to contribute, with employers, to an individual education plan (IEP) specifying the objectives pursued by the student, the education required to obtain a diploma recognised on the labour market, and the necessary work experience.

Many countries seek to enhance the employability of young adults with disabilities by facilitating their entry to vocational education and training courses and/or by matching education courses more closely to the requirements and pressures of the labour market. In particular, Germany has developed a transition system (the *Übergangssystem*) which provides vocational training in a school environment for young adults with disabilities who have had some customised training (*Förderlehrgang*). Measures proposed by the federal employment agency also help to gain entry to employment (Baethge *et al.*, 2007; Schier, 2005). Like other countries, Norway has developed vocational education and training programmes to place young adults in a working environment so that they can acquire useful skills and gain professional experience (OECD, 2006, 2008c). In the United States, the *School to Work Opportunities Act (1994-2001)* led individual states and municipalities to associate educational curricula more closely with the demands of the world of work. In 2010, the United States appropriated USD 1.2 billion to the US Department of Education's Office of Adult and Vocational Education to fund state CTE grants to prepare young adults to meet the demands of the labour market.

France has facilitated access to the vocational education and training stream of upper secondary education and has developed support for accessing vocational and training courses that allow persons with disabilities to acquire the knowledge and skills necessary to find and keep a job. The number of students with disabilities in professional upper secondary schools tripled between 2000 and 2008, to 37.1% of all upper secondary students, while the number of students with disabilities enrolled in EREA has risen tenfold. The number of young adults with disabilities following courses provided by the Adult Vocational Training Agency (*Agence pour la formation professionnelle des adultes* – AFPA) is growing by 10% a year.

Ireland has diversified upper second level education since the mid-1990s to provide a stronger vocational and technical emphasis by offering a wide range of academic and vocational subjects. Two new programmes, the Leaving Certificate Vocational Programme (LCVP) and the Leaving Certificate Applied Programme (LCA), are offered in addition to the established Leaving Certificate in order to widen students' choices. These programmes are pre-vocational in nature. They focus on vocational/technical subjects, preparation for work and work experience (generally a maximum of 20 days). In 2007, Ireland made special arrangements for 2 411 students with disabilities preparing for the leaving certificate applied, nearly ten times as many as in 2003, mainly by granting them exemptions from certain subjects (58%) or giving them reading assistance (30.8%). A further 3 459 students with disabilities received accommodations in the established Leaving Certificate or Leaving Certificate Vocational Programme examinations that year. Specific programmes such as Youthreach offer integrated general education and vocational training programmes for those who have left school early. However, most school leavers now entering vocational education and training courses have first completed upper second level education.

Again, there are few data on conditions of access to vocational education and training courses for secondary school students with disabilities or on outcomes. The data supplied by some countries, however, point to disparities, depending on the type of impairment. In France, students with an intellectual disability are four times more likely, and those with psychological disorders twice as likely, to be enrolled in a professional upper secondary schools rather than in a general ones. Moreover, 63% of EREA students are enrolled in "specialised" EREAs for youngsters with a motor or sensory impairment (ministère de l'Éducation nationale, ministère de l'Enseignement supérieur et de la Recherche, 2010).

Vocational education and training is not always a viable option for young adults with disabilities, although the situation varies between countries and institutions. In Norway, the apprenticeship model (2+2) may be unattractive to them, and many in fact drop out. The sequential schedule, which involves two years of theoretical study followed by two years of practical work experience, may discourage those who find the academic portion too long. Moreover, requiring students with disabilities to find firms for their internships may also lead to failure and dropout, as they may encounter prejudices on the part of employers and employees and thus find it difficult to obtain an internship.

In France, the vocational education and training stream is not very successful at equipping students with the academic knowledge and skills demanded by the labour market. The 2006 PISA score, for example, was 50 points lower, on average, than the score for the general stream (OECD, 2009b). Moreover, schools do not maintain sufficiently close and formal links to the world of work, they do not always give students with disabilities the support they need in their career and educational choices, and they rarely help them find internships that are professionally useful.

In the Czech Republic, nearly 75% of upper secondary students with disabilities are enrolled in special classes, which are often located in special schools that are ill-suited to preparing them for the workplace. Moreover, the division of responsibilities between the Ministry of Education, Youth and Sports and the Ministry of Employment and Social Affairs is not always clearly delineated, and schools do not always make it a priority to prepare students for working life, particularly as students with disabilities may remain in special schools to the age of 25.

In the United States the lack of CTE courses in high schools is a sizable obstacle to the employment of young adults, particularly if they have a disability or a specific learning difficulty. According to the OECD, small learning groups in high schools that combine academic and technical education in a supportive environment improve the employment rate of those at risk of dropping out of education, whereas alternative work-oriented education can offer tailored solutions to help youth facing specific barriers to labour market entry (OECD, 2009c).

Developing synergies by combining academic success with inclusion

Difficulties in accessing employment are a reminder that access to tertiary education does not in itself protect against unemployment. In Ireland the employment rate for disabled young adults with a tertiary education degree falls short by 9% of that for young adults without a disability, while in Norway the equivalent gap was 23.6% in 2008, 5% higher than in 2002 (Figure 4.7).

Figure 4.7. Employment rate of persons with disabilities (aged 16-66) with a tertiary education in Norway compared to the total working population with a tertiary education

Percentage

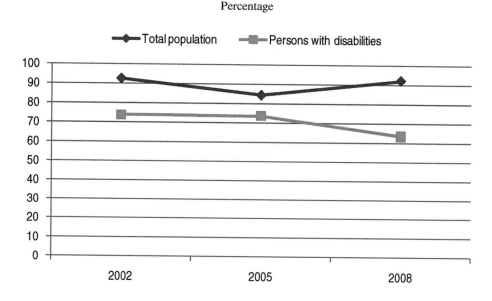

Source: Legard, S. (2009), "Pathways from Education to Work for Young People with Impairments and Learning Difficulties in Norway", Work Research Institute, Oslo.

Facilitate the acquisition of work experience in tertiary education

The existence of ISCED 5B courses or programmes combining school and work segments can be crucial for the most vulnerable students, such as those with disabilities, or those less inclined to take the risk of enrolling in a lengthy course of doubtful professional value. Less theoretical than ISCED 5A courses, they may better suit the aspirations of certain categories of young adults with disabilities, particularly those with a specific learning difficulty. Through a combination of study and work, they help students with disabilities acquire work experience that can be facilitate their subsequent employability. In the United States, for example, students with disabilities registered in business or technical schools were more than three times as likely to have completed their programmes as were those at community colleges and were ten times as likely to finish as were those in tertiary education (Newman *et al.*, 2009).

The existence of bridges or transfer points between vocational (ISCED 5B) and general (ISCED 5A) education at the tertiary level can help to prevent career decisions taken on the completion of secondary education from committing students with disabilities to branches or fields of study that may reduce their scope for choice and compromise their access to employment or their professional development (OECD, 2000).

It reduces the likelihood of failure for students obliged to change courses because of impairment or illness that threatens to halt or disrupt their career. It also encourages the smooth continuation of their career path when they wish to embark on more professionally oriented courses following completion of lower secondary education (Reiersen, 2004). In France, for example, students encountering difficulty or wishing to abandon their course of study have the possibility to switch to more technical courses (*institut universitaire de technologie* – IUT; *section de technicien supérieur* –STS) and thus enhance their chances of success in tertiary education (OECD, 2009a).

Several countries have reinforced the professional dimension of tertiary studies. Norway has created courses that run for six months to two years of instruction and are geared to the evolving needs of the labour market, and in 2007 the Norwegian Confederation of Industry and Commerce (NHO) launched a project to test an apprenticeship scheme in tertiary education whereby students could alternate work and study stints throughout the course. France has extended compulsory work experience and has increased possibilities for school-work combinations by developing professional diplomas (*licences*), which are offered by universities in partnership with business and professional associations and which combine theoretical and practical instruction, practice with methods and tools, a 12-16 week professional work assignment, and completion of a supervised project. In the United States, the *Carl D. Perkins Career and Technical Education Improvement Act of 2006* is intended to improve the employability of young adults with disabilities by encouraging states to ensure them the same access to CTE courses as that of young adults without disabilities. Ireland offers vocational training through the further education and training sector (programmes provided by the National Training and Employment Authority [FAS], Failte Ireland, the Agriculture and Food Development Authority [TEAGASC], REHAB, etc.) and provides an extensive range of vocational training programmes for school leavers and adults that lead to awards delivered by the Further Education and Training Awards Council (FETAC).

Such initiatives seem to have facilitated access to tertiary education for young adults with disabilities in some countries. In the United States, the proportion of students with disabilities attending community colleges is slightly higher than that of other students (13.1% versus 11.8%) and 5% of them take courses offered by career (career-technical) training centres (Getzel *et al.*, 2001; Wagner, 2006a).

In Ireland, the number of students with disabilities in ISCED 5B education has increased by a factor of five in recent years, and in 2008 represented 53% of students with disabilities in tertiary education. In that same year, 11% of students earning a post-leaving certificate had a special education need and many of them found a job upon completion of their course or were able to move on to ISCED 5A training (Higher Education Authority, 2009). For example, half of the students with disabilities tracked by the Further Education College of Limerick took an ISCED 5A course and 40% found a job.

Overall, however, young adults with disabilities are less likely than other young adults to take the professionally most promising courses. In Norway, 52.9% of students with disabilities take ISCED 5B training, while 76% of students without disabilities pursue ISCED 5A courses (Statistics Norway, 2009). In Germany, students with disabilities are more likely to be enrolled in social sciences/pedagogy/psychology (21%) or in mathematics/natural sciences (20%) (Bundesministerium für Bildung und Forschung, 2007). As shown in Table 4.2, in France, they are less likely to be enrolled in the most selective branches of study (engineering, advanced technology) where students can look forward to a low unemployment rate and a comfortable starting salary at work.

They are overrepresented in the human and social sciences (36% versus 32.3%), *i.e.* fields of study that lead to higher unemployment rates (up to 20% in arts and letters), uncertain career paths marked by short-term contracts (two-thirds of jobs offering no notable improvement during the first six years of working life), and pay rates comparable to those for short-cycle diplomas (bac+2) (Ebersold, 2008; OECD, 2009b).

Table 4.2. Type of courses followed by students with disabilities compared with students without disabilities

	France (a) (2007)		United States (b) (2003)	
	No SEN	SEN	No SEN	SEN
Humanities and social sciences	23.7	34.2	16.7	25.6
Law, economics, business	21.0	20.2	15.9	14.9
Science	12.9	17.4	4.4	4.1
Health	9.9	10.2	13.0	12.0
Education, pedagogy, sporting sciences and techniques	5.2	2.2	9.0	8.2
Engineering	5.4	1.4	5.3	3.8
Advanced technology sections (STS), *grandes écoles*	15.9	4.1		
Professional /technical courses	6.0	10.3	2.3	2.9
Total	100.0	100.0	100.0	100.0

SEN = special educational needs.

Source: Author's compilation based on information from (a) Ministère de l'enseignement supérieur et de la recherche. (b) Horn, L. and S. Nevill (2006), *Profile of Undergraduates in U.S. Postsecondary Education Institutions: 2003–04: With a Special Analysis of Community College Students* (NCES 2006-184), US Department of Education, National Center for Education Statistics, Washington, DC.

In France, students with disabilities attending the *grandes écoles* or the advanced technology sections (STS) are more likely than average to have health problems (43.7%) as opposed to a sensory (26.5%) or motor impairment (22.1%); the latter groups tend to enrol in courses or subjects that offer fewer employment opportunities. In the United States, the proportion of young adults with disabilities pursuing vocational education and training is declining in favour of more theoretical courses of study, particularly when they have a speech problem or a specific learning difficulty (Wagner *et al.*, 2006a).

Place more emphasis on employment in tertiary education strategies

Difficulties in obtaining employment also have to do with the importance of employment in the policies of tertiary education institutions.

Important initiatives have been taken in this field. Some countries have developed programmes specifically devoted to the employment of students with disabilities. In Ireland, the Willing Able Mentoring (WAM) programme, created by the Association for Higher Education Access and Disability (AHEAD) and co-financed by the EU EQUAL programme, has helped 47 graduates with disabilities find regular employment. The Norwegian Health Ministry has developed a support programme for regular workplace employment that has benefited 118 students with disabilities, 61% of whom have found a job, and, every year for the last decade, a big telecommunications firm has offered the opportunity for work experience and potential employment to 15 students with a mobility impairment. In Germany, special support and accommodation arrangements allow students with health problems to combine study with an occupation, if they so wish or have a financial need to do so (Deutsches Studentenwerk, 2008).

In the United States, according to the country report, the *American Recovery and Reinvestment Act* (ARRA) has funded programmes of the *Workforce Investment Act* to the equivalent of EUR 3.19 billion, nearly half of which goes to programmes for young adults furthest removed from the labour market. Moreover, the Federal Work Study (FWS) programme offers part-time jobs to students pursuing their studies. The Workforce Recruitment Program for College Students with Disabilities (WRT) allows employers to interview every year more than 1 500 students with disabilities who seek on-the-job experience or employment after their training, and to constitute a file with candidate profiles from more than 200 tertiary education institutions. Nearly 4 500 students have benefited from the programme since its inception in 1995. In 2008-09, the Postsecondary Education, Employment and Research (PEER) project helped 22 persons aged 18-21 with a developmental problem to prepare themselves for the labour market, to be independent on campus, and to be part of the community.

Tertiary education institutions take also specific initiatives to facilitate access to employment for students with disabilities. The Disability Support Service of George Washington University, for example, informs students with disabilities about existing employment possibilities at federal level, advises them on strategies for disclosing information about their disability or their learning difficulty to potential employers, and informs them of the support they may obtain for arranging internships. In Ireland, the Limerick Institute of Technology has established links with the employment facilitation office to help students with disabilities arrange internships. In France, the University of Paris 8 includes disability issues in the sessions it organises for putting students in touch with employers. Aarhus University includes guidance on employment in the training programme it provides for reception and accommodation officers of the Aarhus region, which is financed by the regional authorities.

Nonetheless, students with disabilities remain less likely than other students to find suitable internships or to be able to combine study with work. In the United States, only 18% of students with disabilities who have left high school say that they combine study with work, although the majority of American students do so (Newman *et al.*, 2009). In Norway, many students interviewed considered themselves professionally penalised because they have been unable to pursue either an internship or a job during their course of study or during university vacations, whereas 50% of young adults aged 18-20 engage in an occupation during their studies (OECD, 2008c). French students complain of inadequate support in finding internships, and Irish students felt that the difficulty of arranging internships disadvantaged them professionally upon completion of their training.

Tertiary education institutions are not always as aware of the professional future of students with disabilities as of other students, especially in countries where the diagnostic approach to disability prevails or in which institutions have only recently been encouraged to give employment issues the attention they deserve. Employment for these students is rarely an integral part of university policies for career guidance and placement services, which leave this issue to the disability support and accommodation services. In Denmark, the support offered by the Ministry of Education's disability services is only concerned with access to education and therefore includes internship arrangements. However, it does not include the support students with disabilities may require in order to have a job in parallel to their studies as most Danish students do. In Norway, employment support for students (including those with disabilities) is delegated to student associations and the scope and nature of the service depends, according to persons interviewed, on the number of students enrolled rather than on any institutional strategy.

Disability support services for students with disabilities also pay scant attention to employment in their admission and support strategies. Assessment of support needs takes little account of the student's professional aims, and support staff find it difficult to make internship or sponsorship arrangements with businesses or helping students with disabilities combine study and work part of their mission. They tend to stress the pedagogical and psychological dimensions of support to the detriment of employment issues. Students with disabilities often feel abandoned when they seek an internship, especially if their disability arouses prejudice or if they have to answer detailed questions about the accommodations they would need. Furthermore, disability support services rarely co-operate with the institution's career guidance services. They therefore have trouble building the bridges needed to combine academic and professional success and make employment an integral component of the university's accessibility policy. As a result, employers may complain of a lack of guidance during the internship and a lack of support during the phase of recruitment and integration of young adults with disabilities in the firm.

Closer collaboration with the career guidance centres would improve the quality of employment counselling and support for students with disabilities. Career guidance centres do not always have the skills to counsel students with disabilities properly on the best strategies for disclosing their disability to potential employers, the support to which they and their employers are entitled, or the conditions for implementing special accommodations in the workplace. Moreover, and unlike the employment assistance units created under employment activation policies, career guidance centres seldom provide guidance to those seeking and engaged in employment. At the end of their studies, students with disabilities may therefore have the disconcerting feeling of "falling off of a cliff", and tertiary education institutions deprive themselves of the chance to forge links with a view to the placement of all their students. Some employers may complain that students do not disclose their disability or their specific learning difficulty in time, place too much stress on incapacities due to their disability to the detriment of the skills they have acquired, are insufficiently prepared for the job and lack self-confidence.

Reinforce synergies between tertiary education and firms

Create and formalise links with employers

Difficulties for obtaining employment reflect the isolation of tertiary education institutions from their environment, especially from employers. On the whole, universities have strengthened their ties to employers, although the extent and form of these ties vary. Montgomery College seeks to help employers find the best-qualified candidates for the jobs available. It allows businesses to post their job offers on its Internet site and to meet with students during events devoted to internships or recruitment. In Norway, some businesses have established ties with the University of Oslo which have facilitated employment for many students. Over ten years, its ties to a big Norwegian telecommunications company have resulted in jobs for around 100 students with impaired mobility. Links with businesses can also make it easier for students with disabilities to arrange internships. In France, interns recruited for more than 150 hours can be counted towards the company's mandatory quota of employees with disabilities, and the attendant special accommodation and transport costs are covered by the Organisation for the management of the fund for the professional integration of persons with disabilities (*Association de gestion du fonds pour l'insertion professionnelle des personnes handicapées* – AGEPFIPH) or the Fund for the employment of persons with disabilities in the civil service (*Fonds pour l'insertion des personnes handicapées dans la fonction publique* – FIPHFP).

These linkages, however, do not seem sufficiently strong or permanent, especially in universities, to take full advantage of initiatives to encourage businesses to recruit persons with disabilities. Ireland, for example, offers financial support to businesses that hire a person with disabilities for more than 20 hours a week to offset any productivity loss beyond 20% and to cover the additional costs of accommodating the employee, as well as the costs of hiring a disability support officer when firms recruit more than 30 persons with disabilities. France requires private and public sector employers to recruit a quota of employees with disabilities, and it provides financial, technical and methodological support for this purpose. Denmark has taken steps to help businesses increase their proportion of employees with disabilities by 1% a year.

These initiatives have encouraged many employers to recruit persons with disabilities and to introduce policies in favour of diversity. Universities, however, seem to have difficulty responding to enterprises' request and some businesses interviewed mentioned that they had little contact with the university employment services, while others reported that it was hard to contact students with disabilities for recruitment purposes.

Improve co-operation with the employment support services

Links between universities and employment placement services created as part of active labour market policies are also too informal and too weak. All countries have now taken steps to promote the employment of persons with disabilities as part of their active employment policies. Ireland, for example, quadrupled (to EUR 74 million) the funding devoted to their placement in regular jobs between 2001 and 2008, and the number of beneficiaries increased by nearly 30% between 2003 and 2008 (Higher Education Authority, 2009). In particular, it has created programmes for young adults with disabilities who are nearing employment but need individualised support and coaching and some initial experience in a work situation. For its part, the National Learning Network offers individualised training to strengthen technical, physical and psychological skills along with evaluation and support services for persons with learning or behavioural difficulties.

France has set up a network of placement bodies to assist employers with recruitment procedures and to help persons with disabilities to obtain employment. It more than doubled the offer of training for persons with disabilities between 1998 and 2006, and measures to facilitate access to employment rose by 9% over the period to 20.8%.

Denmark has developed measures to facilitate access to employment and vocational education and training for persons with disabilities, with the goal of 2 000 job placements a year. It has created a specialised centre to provide coaching and support to employment advisory services, offer information on legislation and ways of optimising employment access for young adults with disabilities, and develop new methods to help them become part of the regular workforce. It has also introduced a financial support programme for young graduates facing employment difficulties, to help them obtain work experience, and another to provide them with the services of a workplace assistant.

The Ticket to Work programme in the United States was created in 1999 to provide individuals receiving disability benefits with more choices and opportunities to obtain employment services from public as well as private providers, employers and other organisations. These services include vocational rehabilitation, training and job placement, as well as other support services necessary to achieve a career goal.

The Youth Transition Demonstration (YTD) project of the US Social Security Administration (SSA) provides support to youth with disabilities for accessing employment and other services by empowering them and their families to be more proactive in their approach to the transition from youth to adulthood and by creating integrated co-ordination systems (Figure 4.8). It seeks to better articulate the relationship between general and vocational education and training, to strengthen the links between the education system and other sectors in order to make transitions to employment and tertiary education as smooth and flexible as possible, and to mobilise the social and health services to assist young adults with disabilities at work, in the classroom and in the community. Job development specialists contact and counsel employers, coach young adults in finding employment, and help them settle into their job.

The links between tertiary education institutions, especially universities, and employment services for young adults with disabilities are relatively weak. Information sites only occasionally have links to available employment services and support for jobseekers. For example, few French universities have links to the employment network (*CAP emploi*), which is responsible for improving access to employment for persons with disabilities, or to guidance centres at local level (*missions locales*). This makes the access of young adults with disabilities to vocational education and training courses quite complex. In Norway, examples of co-operation between the Norwegian Labour and Welfare Organisation (NAV) and the universities and projects recently developed by NAV to foster employment opportunities of students with disabilities have been hampered by problems encountered by career guidance centres for identifying eligible students and advising them properly. Only a quarter of American high schools contact universities, vocational education and training institutes or job placement services in connection with the transition plan worked out with students with disabilities, and too little has been done to develop formal links between schools and universities, local education authorities, local services and employment services (Cobb and Alwell, 2007; Wagner *et al.*, 2006b). George Washington University's links to the Washington Center for Internships and Academic Seminars are of special interest in this regard in that scholarships of up to EUR 6 900 are offered for the most deserving students with disabilities wishing to gain work experience with the federal government in the executive, legislative and judicial branches. These services also help students with disabilities contact potential employers and give employers the chance to find qualified and competent workers.

Figure 4.8. The Youth Transition Demonstration project of the US Social Security Administration

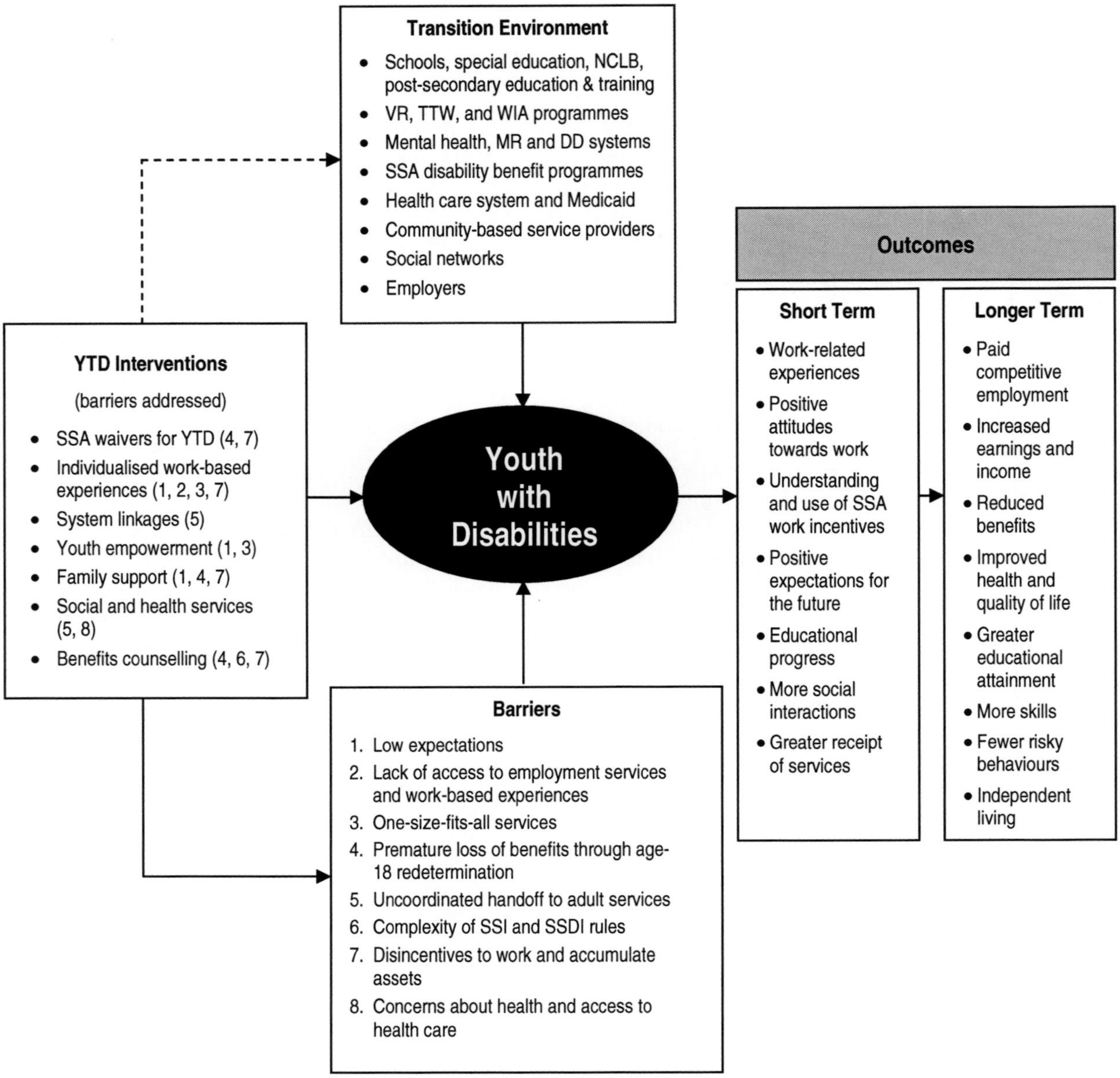

Transition Environment

- Schools, special education, NCLB, post-secondary education & training
- VR, TTW, and WIA programmes
- Mental health, MR and DD systems
- SSA disability benefit programmes
- Health care system and Medicaid
- Community-based service providers
- Social networks
- Employers

YTD Interventions

(barriers addressed)

- SSA waivers for YTD (4, 7)
- Individualised work-based experiences (1, 2, 3, 7)
- System linkages (5)
- Youth empowerment (1, 3)
- Family support (1, 4, 7)
- Social and health services (5, 8)
- Benefits counselling (4, 6, 7)

Youth with Disabilities

Barriers

1. Low expectations
2. Lack of access to employment services and work-based experiences
3. One-size-fits-all services
4. Premature loss of benefits through age-18 redetermination
5. Uncoordinated handoff to adult services
6. Complexity of SSI and SSDI rules
7. Disincentives to work and accumulate assets
8. Concerns about health and access to health care

Outcomes

Short Term

- Work-related experiences
- Positive attitudes towards work
- Understanding and use of SSA work incentives
- Positive expectations for the future
- Educational progress
- More social interactions
- Greater receipt of services

Longer Term

- Paid competitive employment
- Increased earnings and income
- Reduced benefits
- Improved health and quality of life
- Greater educational attainment
- More skills
- Fewer risky behaviours
- Independent living

Source: US Department of Education, Office of Special Education and Rehabilitative Services, Office of Special Education Programs (2010), "Pathways for Students with Disabilities to Tertiary Education and Employment", Country background report, Washington, DC.

Yet tertiary education institutions do not always work with their environment sufficiently closely, and the exchanges that exist do not always lead to the kind of co-operation that would produce the synergies for combining academic success and access to employment. University career services in Denmark, for example, rarely have staff specialised in access to employment for students with disabilities, who may therefore lack the support that would facilitate their access to internships, help them combine study and work, and find a job upon completing their course of study. In Norway, the lack of communication between universities and employers may deprive students with disabilities of the chance to make use of government-sponsored formulas for testing their capacities. Disability support services lack the tools for including employment issues in their admissions and support strategies, and students with disabilities may encounter real difficulties in finding a job.

The disability employment services created in the context of active employment policies may tend to overlook the difficulties faced by students with disabilities who are enrolled in tertiary education. They may also have trouble taking over from the education system when it comes to making adapted workplace arrangements and creating the conditions for the transition from tertiary education to employment. As noted during the onsite visits, they may misinterpret the reluctance of students with an invisible disability (a behavioural or psychological disorder) to disclose their situation and to apply for the employment assistance for which they are eligible.

Conclusion

The rise in enrolments in tertiary education among students with disabilities has a limited impact on their subsequent employment. Young adults with disabilities remain overexposed to unemployment and exclusion. This may be because recruitment strategies take more and more account of behavioural dimensions and therefore reduce employment opportunities for young adults with disabilities, especially if they have behavioural or mental health difficulties.

It may also be related to the difficulties young adults with disabilities encounter in the education system for access to courses that are professionally promising and prepare them to meet labour market requirements, in a context that makes a diploma essential for employment but insufficient in itself. In upper secondary education, young adults with disabilities may not have easy access to recent initiatives to develop vocational training opportunities and vocational training courses may not be adapted to their needs. As a result, upper secondary students with disabilities may have difficulty accessing vocational training opportunities of good quality which can help them meet labour market requirements.

For their part, despite initiatives to professionalise tertiary education and to create bridges between ISCED 5B and ISCED 5A courses, tertiary education institutions find it difficult to link academic success to professional inclusion. Employment opportunities beyond tertiary education for students with disabilities do not always have the same priority level as for non-disabled students, and admissions and guidance strategies rarely address this issue. In addition, links between tertiary education institutions and employers may sometimes be too weak or too informal and admissions and support services may not work closely enough with universities' career centres or with employment services created under active labour market policies to develop synergies that foster employment opportunities for students with disabilities. As a result, students with disabilities enrolled in tertiary education have difficulty gaining work experience during their studies and accessing internships and may feel isolated once they leave tertiary education; for their part, employers fail to find the qualified employees with disabilities they wish to hire.

Fostering employment opportunities beyond tertiary education requires better inclusion of employment issues in tertiary education institutions' strategies and strengthening of synergies with employers and employment services as a way to foster institutional policies that make access to employment an essential component of the institution's mission.

References

Amar, M. and S. Samira (2003), "L'emploi des personnes handicapées ou ayant des problèmes de santé de longue durée", DARES, *Premières synthèses informations*, No. 41-3.

Baethge, M., S. Solga and M. Wieck (2007), *Berufsbildung im Umbruch – Signale eines überfälligen Aufbruchs*, Friedrich-Ebert-Stiftung, Bonn/Berlin.

Berthoud, R. (2006), *The Employment Rates of Disabled People*, Research Report No. 298, HMSO, London.

Bjerkan, K.Y. and M. Veenstra (2008), "Utdanning, arbeid, bolig og transport for unge voksne 20 til 35 år", *Statusrapport 08: samfunnsutviklingen for personer med nedsatt funksjonsevne*, Nasjonalt dokumentasjonssenter for personer med nedsatt funksjonsevne, Oslo, pp. 154-207.

Bundesministerium für Bildung und Forschung (2007), *Die wirtschaftliche und soziale Lage der Studierenden in der Bundesrepublik Deutschland 2006*; 18. Sozialerhebung des Deutschen Studentenwerks durchgeführt durch HIS Hochschul-Informations-System, Bonn/Berlin.

Central Statistics Office (2008), *National Disability Survey 2006 – First Results,* Dublin Stationery Office.

Cobb, B. and M. Alwell (2007), *Transition Planning/Co-ordinating Interventions for Youth with Disabilities: A Systematic Review,* NSTTAC.

Délégation ministérielle à l'emploi des personnes handicapées (2009), "Parcours des personnes handicapées vers l'enseignement supérieur et vers l'emploi", Country background report France, Ministère de l'éducation nationale, Paris.

Deutsches Studentenwerk (2008), *18. Sozialerhebung des Deutschen Studentenwerks. Die wirtschaftliche und soziale Lage der Studierenden in der Bundesrepublik Deutschland,* Deutsches Studentenwerk, Berlin.

Disabled World (2010), *U.S. Bureau of Labor Statistics Employment Status of Persons with a Disability in the United States,* *http://disabled-world.com/disability/statistics/disability-employment-statistics.php*.

Ebersold, S. (2008), "Adapting Higher Education to the Needs of Disabled Students: Developments, Challenges and Prospects", in OECD, *Higher Education to 2030, Volume 1: Demography*, OECD, Paris.

Getzel, E.E., R.A. Stodden and L.W. Briel (2001), "Pursuing Postsecondary Education Opportunities for Individuals with Disabilities", in P. Wehman (ed.), *Life Beyond the Classroom: Transition Strategies for Young People with Disabilities,* Paul H. Brookes Publishing Co., Baltimore, MD.

Higher Education Authority (2009), *Higher Education Key Facts and Figures 07/08*, Dublin.

Horn, L. and S. Nevill (2006), *Profile of Undergraduates in U.S. Postsecondary Education Institutions: 2003–04: With a Special Analysis of Community College Students* (NCES 2006-184), US Department of Education, National Center for Education Statistics, Washington, DC.

Kuczera, M. (2010), *Learning for Jobs, OECD Reviews of Vocational, Education and Training, Czech Republic,* OECD, Paris.

Legard, S. (2009), "Pathways from Education to Work for Young People with Impairments and Learning Difficulties in Norway", Work Research Institute, Oslo.

Ministère de l'Éducation nationale, ministère de l'Enseignement supérieur et de la Recherche (2010), *Repères et références statistiques sur les enseignements, la formation et la recherche,* La documentation française, Paris.

Ministry of Education of the Czech Republic (2009), "Transitions to Tertiary Education and to Employment for Young People with Impairments and Learning Difficulties", Country background report, Ministry of Education of the Czech Republic, Prague.

Newman, L. *et al.* (2009), *The Post-High School Outcomes of Youth with Disabilities up to 4 Years After High School,* SRI International, Menlo Park, CA.

Nguyen, K.N. and V. Ulrich (2008), "L'accès à l'emploi des personnes handicapées en 2007", *Premières informations sociales*, DARES, No. 47.1.

OECD (2000), *From Initial Education to Working Life: Making Transitions Work*, OECD, Paris.

OECD (2003), *Transforming Disability into Ability: Policies to Promote Work and Income Security for Disabled People*, OECD, Paris.

OECD (2006), *Sickness, Disability and Work: Breaking the Barriers, Volume 1: Norway, Poland and Switzerland*, OECD, Paris.

OECD (2008a), *Sickness, Disability and Work: Breaking the Barriers, Volume 3: Denmark, Finland, Ireland and the Netherlands*, OECD, Paris.

OECD (2008b), *OECD Employment Outlook*, OECD, Paris.

OECD (2008c), *Jobs for Youth/Des emplois pour les jeunes: Norway*, OECD, Paris.

OECD (2009a), *Education at a Glance*, OECD, Paris.

OECD (2009b), *Jobs for Youth/Des emplois pour les jeunes: France*, OECD, Paris.

OECD (2009c), *Jobs for Youth/Des emplois pour les jeunes: United States*, OECD, Paris.

OECD (2010), *Jobs for Youth/Des emplois pour les jeunes: Denmark*, OECD, Paris.

Powell, J.J.W, K. Felkendorff and J. Hollenweger (2008), "Disability in the German, Swiss and Austrian Education Systems", S.L. Gabel and S. Danforth (eds.), *Disability and the Politics of Education*, Peter Lang, New York.

Reiersen, T. (2004), *Oppfølgingsundersøkelse av arbeidssøkere som sluttet å melde seg ved Aetat høsten 2002*, Del 2: Yrkeshemmede arbeidssøkere.

Schier, F. (2005), "Wege der beruflichen Bildung junger Menschen mit Behinderung im dualen System", in R. Bieker (ed.), *Teilhabe am Arbeitsleben. Wege der beruflichen Integration von Menschen mit Behinderung,* Kohlhammer Verlag, Stuttgart, pp. 148-166.

Statistics Norway (2009), *Fakta om utdanning I Norge 2009: nokkeltall fra 2007,* Statistic sentralbyrå, Oslo.

US Department of Education, Office of Special Education and Rehabilitative Services, Office of Special Education Programs (2010), "Pathways for Students with Disabilities to Tertiary Education and Employment", Washington, DC.

US Department of Labor (2010), *Persons with a Disability: Labor Force Characteristics 2009,* Bureau of Labor Statistics, *www.bls.gov/news.release/disabl.nr0.htm.*

Wagner, M. *et al.* (2005), *After High School: A First Look at the Postschool Experiences of Youth with Disabilities, A report from the National Longitudinal Transition Study-2 (NLTS2),* SRI International, Menlo Park, CA.

Wagner, M. *et al.* (2006a), *The Academic Achievement and Functional Performance of Youth with Disabilities. A Report of Findings from the National Longitudinal Study-2 (NLTS2),* SRI International, Menlo Park, CA.

Wagner, M. *et al.* (2006b), *An Overview of Findings From Wave 2 of the National Longitudinal Transition Study-2 (NLTS2),* SRI International, Menlo Park, CA.

Chapter 5

Conclusions and Recommendations

Access to tertiary education for young adults with disabilities, particularly for those with learning difficulties, has improved significantly over the past decade in the countries participating in the project (the Czech Republic, Denmark, France, Norway, Ireland, the United States). This reflects the growing number of young adults with disabilities with the prerequisites for tertiary education as a result of policies to promote the inclusion of disabled people developed over the past 20 years.

The "school for all" has increased access to tertiary education

This increase illustrates the promotion of a "school for all" which seeks to be both efficient and equitable and to facilitate the participation of all in the economic and social development of society.

The "school for all" mobilises financial, technical and human resources to provide students with disabilities equal opportunities on an equal footing with their peers by compensating for the consequences of their disability. Financial and methodological incentives have encouraged schools to be receptive to the diversity of educational profiles and have prompted tertiary education institutions to incorporate impairment in their institution's policy and to provide admissions and support services for students with disabilities.

The "school for all" makes the educational success of every student, regardless of his or her particularities, one of its goals and makes academic excellence the means of supporting the weakest while encouraging the strongest. The development of universal design learning environments flexible enough to be adapted to the diversity of educational needs, the reduction of dropout rates, and quality assurance policies have all helped to increase the number of students with disabilities able to aspire to tertiary education.

In addition, the growing number of students with disabilities in tertiary education reflects the growing mobilisation of educational systems around students' prospects, through the diversification of educational opportunities on the completion of upper secondary education, the creation of the bridges to ease the transition into the various pathways between levels and educational sectors, and the existence of measures offering exemptions to disadvantaged groups, including disabled pupils and students.

Institutions' strategies determine access to tertiary education

The growing proportion of young adults with disabilities in tertiary education is a direct result of the strategies adopted by upper secondary schools and tertiary education institutions to build pathways to tertiary education and prepare upper secondary school students to cope with the demands of the transition to adulthood.

The strategies developed by secondary schools generally aim to provide upper secondary school students with disabilities with the information that will allow them to make informed decisions on the basis of their capacities and professional aspirations. Less often, they encourage students to plan carefully and sufficiently in advance the steps along the path to tertiary education, while few are designed to prepare them to cope with the demands that will be placed on them at the end of their secondary education.

In tertiary education, admission and support strategies, although they vary from one institution to another, are designed to prompt students with disabilities to involve themselves actively in their chosen courses and to encourage the institution to ensure that such students are successful and integrated into the university community.

To this end, they seek to reduce risks of failure by forging links with services that deal with extracurricular dimensions (transport, housing) or by extending the work done in secondary education. Institutions can take part in open days or information fairs, for example, forge links with staff from secondary education institutions or offer pathways to allow students to link their choices to a project and to start outlining a roadmap for the transition process.

Admissions strategies also tend to make students with disabilities responsible for themselves. They encourage them to mention their educational needs at as early a stage as possible so that the necessary arrangements and support can be prepared beforehand. They also advise students on the organisation of courses, inform them about their accessibility policy and the support and accommodations which they can expect. They raise their awareness of the implications of their choices in terms of academic requirements.

In addition, admissions strategies also aim to forge a contractual relationship with students with disabilities that can mobilise actors within the institution around a support plan that specifies the objectives pursued, the support and accommodations needed, and the conditions for their implementation.

An inclusive ethos facilitates transition

The quality of the transition process depends on the existence of an inclusive ethos at the level of the institution which makes openness to diversity one of its goals and pedagogical, social, psychological and physical accessibility a component of the institution's culture.

This inclusive ethos is predicated on making the university community aware of the role that diversity can play as a driver of innovation and creativity and of the counterproductive effect of prejudice against young adults with disabilities. It is also based on mobilising each member of the institution to ensure the success of individual students through training courses on inclusive education, by putting forward role models to rally the community and by promoting peer support.

This inclusive ethos can be seen particularly clearly in countries that have adopted an educational approach to disability which primarily encourages relating the difficulties faced by students with disabilities to institutions' modes of organisation and to teachers' pedagogical practices. Institutions in such countries tend to see diversity as a source of success for the entire university community, to consider support and accommodations as a way to facilitate the success of every student and to view accessibility as a source of development.

Where a diagnostic approach to disability prevails, tertiary education institutions tend to see diversity as the exception; they also perceive the presence of students with disabilities as a constraint and the provision of special arrangements and support as an additional cost.

Disabled students have a harder and bumpier
transition to tertiary education

Despite the progress made, access to tertiary education for young students with disabilities, particularly those with an impairment (sensory, motor or mental) or psychological problems, nonetheless continues to be more difficult than for other young adults. For example, while the general rate of entry to tertiary education in Ireland rose by 8% between 2000 and 2006, the country report states that the increase for disabled persons was merely 2.6%.

The pathways of young adults with disabilities to tertiary education are also less straightforward than those of other young adults. There may be gaps along the way, resulting in breaks or forced changes of direction. In Norway, the country report noted that 24% of students with disabilities claimed not to have been able to follow their first choice of course.

Students with disabilities are also less likely than their non-disabled peers to complete their studies successfully, particularly when they have a specific learning difficulty, behavioural difficulties or psychological problems.

Transitions policies have expanded access
opportunities but do not address all the
obstacles that students face

In recent years transition policies have significantly expanded opportunities for access to and success in tertiary education for young adults with disabilities, especially among those with a specific learning difficulty. However, they have not always taken sufficient account of the factors that facilitate continuity and coherence along the path to tertiary education and employment. They therefore risk leaving the opportunity to enter higher education and employment to the individuals concerned and to their families. They also risk increasing the vulnerability of those with sensory, motor or mental impairments and/or from less fortunate socio-economic backgrounds.

They have also failed to recognise the obstacles that students with disabilities may encounter in the course of their studies. These can overexpose them to dropout at the end of the first year, to failure to complete their programme, or to more complicated itineraries. Moreover, they insufficiently link the financing modalities and additional resources allocated to institutions and to young adults with disabilities to their possibilities for social and professional inclusion. As a result such individuals may remain unemployed or underemployed in spite of easier access to higher education.

Inclusive policies have not always succeeded in ensuring that the transition of young adults with disabilities is integrated in a system able to ensure a safe path forward at the end of secondary education and in tertiary education. Yet the development of policies that encourage a good transition to tertiary education and to employment is essential if education policies are to be efficient and equitable in terms of access, success and a promising future.

Some countries are developing specific transition policies but still face a range of challenges

While the forms of transition have been multiplied and extended over the last two decades, education systems face persistent difficulties for giving concrete form to the right to education for children and adolescents with disabilities and to ensuring their entry into the world of work. As a result, this issue has now taken on greater urgency. The United States and Denmark have developed specific transition policies, and these have become an integral part of the missions of the education system. Ireland and France have recently taken initiatives for securing educational pathways to tertiary education and employment. Norway also appears to be on the way to doing this and the Czech Republic has recognised the importance of the issue.

The role of transition in reinforcing the possibilities of inclusion, in optimising the planning and steering of inclusive policies and in avoiding excessive costs in a context of strong budgetary pressure has been pinpointed as a major issue. Countries continue to face a range of challenges (Table 5.1).

Table 5.1. Main challenges in optimising transition policies and their magnitude in participating countries

+ minor; ++ moderate; +++ important; ++++ crucial

	Czech Republic	Denmark	France	Ireland	Norway	United States
Mobilise stakeholders and systems around the future of young adults with disabilities and prevent them from being irremediably marginalised by discontinuities.	++++	++	+++	+++	+++	+
Promote synergies between systems and stakeholders involved in the transition process to ensure continuity and coherence in the career path.	++++	++	+++	+++	+++	+++
Empower young adults with disabilities and their families to meet the demands of the transition to adulthood and of tertiary education and employment.	++++	+++	+++	+++	+++	+++
Make systems and stakeholders capable of satisfying the requirements imposed by the definition and implementation of transition processes.	++++	+++	+++	+++	+++	+++
Provide the mechanisms and tools necessary for planning policies and monitoring transition processes.	++++	+	+++	+++	+++	++

Quality transition policies are needed to give equal opportunities and treatment for young adults with disabilities

The following recommendations aim at strengthening the capacity of education systems to give young adults with disabilities equal opportunities and treatment in terms of their access, success and future. They take account of a context of budgetary restrictions which calls for optimising the measures adopted by inclusive policies. They relate to the main challenges to be addressed to optimise policies on transition to tertiary education and employment. They also relate to the capacity of secondary and tertiary education institutions to prepare and empower young adults with disabilities to face the demands of the transition to adulthood and the world of work.

The following recommendations presuppose that quality transition policies are those that:

- provide young adults with disabilities, to the extent possible, with the same knowledge and skills as other young adults;

- furnish them, on the same basis as other young adults, with qualifications recognised by tertiary education institutions and the labour market;

- prevent them from being more exposed than other young adults to being neither in employment nor in education or training;

- offer them the same chances of access to the same quality of employment as young adults without disabilities;

- give them equal opportunities in terms of the length and quality of transition.

The aim of these recommendations is to optimise transition opportunities to tertiary education and employment for young adults with disabilities, through policies that:

- are organised around an educational approach to disability which focuses on the enabling or disabling effect of policies and practices rather than treating it as an intrinsic personal characteristic;

- promote a legislative framework that prohibits all forms of discrimination and requires institutions to draw up an annual action plan specific to young adults with disabilities which includes the question of transition;

- ensure that the support offered acts as an incentive for tertiary education and access to employment;

- develop bridges between stakeholders involved in the transition process to tertiary education which foster the continuity and coherence of the paths between educational levels and sectors;

- provide education systems with financial and methodological incentives to improve their transition strategies and strengthen their linkages with their environment, particularly with employers and career services;

- link financial resources more closely to the definition of an individual education plan which includes an individual transition plan, the basis of which is the individual's independence and empowerment;

- are rooted in reliable indicators and statistical data which allow for comparing the situation of young adults with disabilities to that of the general population, for determining the enabling effect of the strategies and practices employed and of the support and arrangements provided, and for evaluating the quality of the paths taken by students with disabilities;

- create or improve co-ordination arrangements to facilitate local synergies among stakeholders in the education, employment, social and health sectors;

- improve initial and continuing training for personnel in the education system and provide them with methodological tools and support.

Secondary education institutions lay the foundation for successful transition

Enhancing opportunities for transition to tertiary education and employment also assumes that secondary education institutions will:

- be concerned for every student's success and include transition in their institutional policy;

- define and implement as early as possible an individual transition plan that encourages students to plan for their future, prepares them for the demands of passage to adulthood, and gives them the skills required for tertiary education and employment;

- make sure that students with disabilities and their families, as well as the different categories of stakeholders concerned, are involved throughout the definition and implementation of the transition process;

- be sufficiently integrated into their local environment to mobilise the resources needed to ensure the quality of the transition process during and at the end of schooling;

- ensure that their arrangements and support are flexible enough to be adapted to the individual needs of students with disabilities;

- have statistics to track the progress of students with disabilities and identify the impact of their arrangements and support;

- ensure that staff members responsible for transition are properly trained and equipped.

Tertiary institutions need to adopt appropriate admission and support policies along with strategies to ensure they work well

Enhancing opportunities for transition to tertiary education and employment also implies that tertiary education institutions will:

- define their admissions and support strategies in co-ordination with secondary schools, non-governmental organisations representing persons with disabilities or parents of persons with disabilities, and the employment sector;

- define a specific policy for students with disabilities which covers the training of staff working in admissions services, the inclusion of representatives of students with disabilities in institutional governance bodies, and awareness raising among staff and students;

- include the employment issue in their admissions and support strategies;

- ensure that disability support services work closely with other student services as well as those that provide support to young adults with disabilities in extracurricular activities;

- include distance education and new technologies in their policy;

- establish and formalise links with employers and employment support services to take advantage of existing initiatives to promote employment of young adults with disabilities.

Access to tertiary education does not necessarily lead to employment

---

The growing presence of students with disabilities in tertiary education only partly translates into successful entry into the labour market. The rate of employment of young adults with disabilities is lower than that of the working population of the same age.

These students' difficulty in gaining access to employment leaves them overexposed to unemployment and exclusion, a trend that is increasing in some countries. It may be due to a growing demand for qualifications, as this particularly penalises young adults with cognitive impairments, and to the growing importance attached by employers to behavioural aspects. It may also reflect certain weaknesses in policies designed to promote access to the labour market.

Gaining work experience while studying is a key element that can facilitate future labour market success

---

However, it also illustrates the difficulties young adults with disabilities face for gaining access to potentially rewarding professional training, given the fact that, while diplomas have become increasingly important, they are no longer sufficient to obtain a job.

Optimising the transition to employment presupposes that:

- the vocational education and training initiatives undertaken in secondary education to optimise the employability of young adults with disabilities offer a real educational alternative;

- tertiary education institutions attach the same importance to the professional future of students with disabilities as they do for other students;

- tertiary education institutions create sufficiently deep-rooted and formalised links with the economic sphere and the actors involved in active employment policies to be able to make full use of initiatives to encourage firms to recruit workers with disabilities;

- admissions and support services for students with disabilities give greater attention to access to employment in their strategies and work more closely with agencies that assist with job searches for persons with disabilities or job placement agencies.

Such initiatives would allow students with disabilities to acquire work experience while studying. They would also mean that at the end of their studies, students would not be facing a leap into the unknown, a situation that can be destabilising for young adults with disabilities. These initiatives would also encourage potential employers and lead to stronger links between tertiary education institutions and the professional world.

Annex

Methodology

Guidelines for the country background reports

National authorities of participating countries are responsible for the preparation of a country report. Its purpose is to identify transition policies with respect to the situation of persons with disabilities or learning difficulties. All country reports used a common framework in order to facilitate comparative analysis and to maximise the opportunities for participating countries to share and learn from each other.

In order to present their transition policies, participating countries were asked to describe the context, their current policies and provision, and the key factors that influence these policies. Countries also highlighted the strengths and weaknesses of their transition policies. The reports covered the following nine topics:

1. definitions of disability

2. data

3. policy

4. funding

5. provision

6. support services

7. training

8. parental and community involvement

9. future developments.

In addition, countries highlighted anticipated trends in future policy developments both in the short and long term and indicate their highest priorities for future development in order to facilitate the transition of persons with disabilities or learning difficulties to tertiary education and/or to employment.

Country reports are based on:

- a literature review covering the factors that facilitate or hinder transition to tertiary education or employment for persons with disabilities or learning difficulties;

- an account of national policies;

- visits and interviews allowing for comparisons between national policies and the actual practices.

The guidelines asked countries to provide comparisons or information on trends over a period of time, generally ten years.

Procedures for preparing the country report

National authorities were responsible for the preparation of the country report. Each participating country appointed a national resource person who co-ordinated the project at national administrative level, attended OECD meetings twice a year and, if required, meetings organised at national level. With respect to the country report, the resource person was responsible for:

- managing the preparation of the country report;

- communications with the OECD about the country report;

- liaising with other ministries that may be concerned by transition issues;

- ensuring the involvement of key stakeholder groups;[1]

- communications within the country about the country report;

- ensuring that the country report was completed on schedule;

- liaising with the OECD about the organisation and the implementation of the visits and the interviews.

Topics covered in the country reports

Topic 1: Definitions of disability

This section showed any differences that may exist between the definition of disability for children and for adults. It also indicated the consequences of these differences for individual with respect to the access to rights, aids and support as well as their continuity. In addition, it highlighted any effects that differences in definition might have with respect to transition to tertiary education and to employment.

Topic 2: Data

This section presented the data available on young persons[2] with disabilities or learning difficulties and the data that was missing, as well as the data collection procedure. It also presented existing data on the situation of young persons with disabilities or learning difficulties in comparison with the average population as well as trends over the last ten years. The data description could include:

- the number of young adults with disabilities or learning difficulties in tertiary education, in vocational education and training, in adult and continuing education, in short-term training, in remedial training, and in employer-based training compared to the number of young adults without disabilities in these situations;

---

1.   These vary from country to country, but would normally include, in addition to the Ministry of Education, responsible ministries in areas such as finance, labour, industry, research, science and technology; employers and trade unions; representatives of academic staff; organisations for students with disabilities; and agencies responsible for funding and quality assurance.

2.   Although the definition of young persons may vary among countries, the data included persons with disabilities or learning difficulties aged 16-30.

- the unemployment rate of young persons with disabilities or learning difficulties compared to the unemployment rate of young adults without disabilities;

- the number of young persons with disabilities or learning difficulties who are not studying and not working compared to the number of young adults without disabilities;

- the employment rate of young persons with disabilities or learning difficulties compared to that of young adults without disabilities;

- the kinds of employment to which young persons with disabilities or learning difficulties have access (type of work, number of working hours, salary) compared to those for young adults without disabilities;

- the number of young persons with disabilities or learning difficulties not undertaking further education after compulsory school compared to the number of young adults without disabilities;

- the level of training and qualification of young persons with disabilities or learning difficulties compared to that of young adults without disabilities.

The data description also presented, when possible, existing data on the performance of the education system, such as:

- the number of students with disabilities or learning difficulties entering and in ISCED 3A and ISCED 3B courses;

- the number of students with disabilities or learning difficulties entering and in ISCED 5A and ISCED 5B courses;

- the number of students with disabilities and learning difficulties who enter tertiary education or employment after secondary education;

- the number of students with disabilities or learning difficulties who enter employment after tertiary education;

- the number of students with disabilities or learning difficulties who remain in tertiary education;

- the success and failures rates of students with disabilities or learning difficulties who had remedial courses.

All data referred, when possible, to the characteristics of the students (type of disability, gender, age, socio-economic status, ethnic minority background).

Topic 3: Policy

The policy description provided the current government policy statements and goals relevant to transition to tertiary education and to employment of those with disabilities and learning difficulties. These policy statements concern social, employment and education policies and may come from single departments – employment, education, health or social welfare, for example – or they may be the result of inter-departmental collaboration. They cover the objectives, the ways in which they are set, the actors involved in setting them, and the tensions that may exist for their implementation.

This section presented existing legislation relevant to the transition to tertiary education and to the employment of persons with disabilities or learning difficulties. It described legislation prohibiting discrimination, legislation and initiatives favouring accessibility of school buildings and universities, promoting training of teaching and administrative staff, and supporting access to vocational education and training and/or workplaces. The description of existing legislation also covered assessment procedures and the extra support disabled students may obtain (time for exams, proximity to students' home, short courses, modularisation, etc.). It also covered changes in legislation with respect to age and disability.

It also included how policies promote accessibility settings for postsecondary education (tertiary education institutions, vocational training centres) as well as policies promoting access to professional life.

This section also provided information on measures taken to link employment, education and health issues. It highlighted how policies promote linkages between upper secondary institutions and tertiary institutions as well as linkages between tertiary education and other forms of education such as vocational education and training, adult and continuing education, short-term job training, remedial training and employer-based training. It described how policies aim to involve employers in the education and training process (financial incentives for employers, availability of methodological, technical and human help for firms and employees).

Topic 4: Funding

This section presented national funding for the education and the transition to tertiary education and to employment of those with disabilities and learning difficulties in addition to the funding allocated for those without any disability or learning difficulty. It covered existing aids for students as well as institutions or families and described eligibility criteria and links between aids and tuition.

Topic 5: Provision

This section described existing systems with regard to employment, education, health, vocational education and training and lifelong education. The description covered existing provision and programmes to encourage people with disabilities or learning difficulties to become actively involved in professional and social life, those that support employers' involvement and those favouring relationships between employment, education and health services.

The description also highlighted the modes of funding, the agencies responsible for funding institutions and individuals and for assuring the system's quality, requirements for students (tuition), assessment procedures, modes of evaluation of the provision, etc.

It discussed in addition any curriculum development work designed to enhance educational organisation, materials, teaching methods or other support for children and students with disabilities or learning difficulties. It described the mechanisms created to improve quality of provision and the existing evidence on this issue.

Topic 6: Support services

This section dealt with the types of structures and support services available to those with disabilities and learning difficulties in the education system, those that serve to link health, education and employment issues, and those devoted to support during the transition to tertiary education, to vocational education and training and to employment. It indicated how students access information, the opportunities available in secondary education and tertiary education, as well as the opportunities for transition between programmes and institutions. It gave information about the roles and added value of academic and non-academic counselling and guidance services, of transition support services, remedial courses and external support services.

The description also covered materials or initiatives designed to assist faculty and staff in working with persons with disabilities or learning difficulties (faculty/staff handbook, annual mailing to faculty/staff, workshops and presentation to faculty groups, one-on-one discussions with faculty staff/staff who request information or assistance, information resources such as books and videotapes for faculty staff). It also described the mechanisms implemented to improve the quality of support.

Topic 7: Training

This section described the extent to which initial and/or in-service training for teachers and other professionals includes information on transition issues as well as any training or other forms of support for non-professionals, notably parents.

Topic 8: Parental and community involvement

This section presented the extent and nature of involvement of parents in the transition process to tertiary education and to employment, as well as initiatives taken in this area. It covered the involvement of voluntary bodies concerned with disabilities as well as other forms of community support, *e.g.* donations by charities or sponsorship by commercial organisations.

Topic 9: Future developments

This section discussed the strengths and weaknesses of existing transition policies and presented the further developments needed and those likely to occur in practice, *e.g.* over the next year or so.

Country visits

The site visits aimed at complementing the information contained in the country reports by taking into account the points of view of various stakeholders.

Procedure

The site visits lasted three to four days during which stakeholders who play a role in the transition of young people with disabilities from upper secondary education to tertiary education and to employment were interviewed. Stakeholders were identified by participating countries which also, in conjunction with the OECD, prepared an agenda for the visit and made the necessary arrangements. Stakeholders included:

- ministers and/or senior officials in ministries/departments of education, employment and health;
- representatives of employers and trade unions;
- representatives of non-governmental organisations (NGOs);

- staff of schools and universities;

- students in schools and universities;

- staff of service providers.

Topics covered

Interviews focused on the strengths and weaknesses of existing policies and practices as well as on factors for improvement. Information was gathered on:

- the implementation of current legislation and policies on transition issues;

- incentives (funding, training, technical support) developed to empower schools, tertiary education institutions, companies and disability support/transition services to implement high-quality transition programmes and how they facilitate or impede cross-sectoral approaches and effective transition;

- incentives (funding, supports, and benefits) developed to empower students with special needs to go on to tertiary education and to employment;

- policies developed by schools and tertiary education institutions to foster continuity of educational pathways with regard to admission procedures, information systems, needs assessments, support, family involvement, collaboration between settings and between departments, etc.

- policies and strategies developed by schools and tertiary education institutions to create links with the employment sector as well as with disability support/transition services;

- policies and strategies developed by employers and disability support/transition services to create links with education sector.

In order to improve the quality of interviews, these were carried out jointly by the OECD and, as far as possible, by a representative of the research centre appointed by the country.

ORGANISATION FOR ECONOMIC CO-OPERATION AND DEVELOPMENT

The OECD is a unique forum where governments work together to address the economic, social and environmental challenges of globalisation. The OECD is also at the forefront of efforts to understand and to help governments respond to new developments and concerns, such as corporate governance, the information economy and the challenges of an ageing population. The Organisation provides a setting where governments can compare policy experiences, seek answers to common problems, identify good practice and work to co-ordinate domestic and international policies.

The OECD member countries are: Australia, Austria, Belgium, Canada, Chile, the Czech Republic, Denmark, Estonia, Finland, France, Germany, Greece, Hungary, Iceland, Ireland, Israel, Italy, Japan, Korea, Luxembourg, Mexico, the Netherlands, New Zealand, Norway, Poland, Portugal, the Slovak Republic, Slovenia, Spain, Sweden, Switzerland, Turkey, the United Kingdom and the United States. The European Union takes part in the work of the OECD.

OECD Publishing disseminates widely the results of the Organisation's statistics gathering and research on economic, social and environmental issues, as well as the conventions, guidelines and standards agreed by its members.

OECD PUBLISHING, 2, rue André-Pascal, 75775 PARIS CEDEX 16
(91 2011 01 1 P) ISBN 978-92-64-09741-4 – No. 58073 2011-01